W9-CWL-842

How did Minnesota—a distant, isolated American state—and its Twin Cities business community become known world-wide for the citizenship and integrity of its corporations and corporate leaders? Natives sometimes weary of reminders of Minnesota's reputation, but the fact remains that leaders from cities across the United States and delegations from Europe, Asia and the Americas keep singing Minnesota's praise and asking how did you do it. Putting together the pieces of that puzzle is the challenge undertaken by Wilfred Bockelman as he weaves Minnesota's thought-provoking story in *Culture of Corporate Citizenship*.

Bockelman understands that cultures are not created overnight. He has reached back across the decades interviewing corporate community leaders, tapping into their perspectives and striving to understand the roots of their commitment to this concept of corporate social responsibility.

The story is not only one of origins and roots. The book is aptly subtitled *Minnesota's Business Legacy for the Global Future.* In an era of protest against free trade, NAFTA, the World Trade Organization, and the World Bank, we are compelled to think about the responsibilities that any business has to address the profound social, civil and environmental challenges arising out of rapid globalization. Can the tools of corporate citizenship developed out of a commitment to one's own immediate community and stakeholders serve us in this new age of multi-nationals stretching across innumerable national and cultural boundaries? Bockelman doesn't shrink from the questions.

Embedded in this tale is the emergence of a nonprofit business organization—the Minnesota Center for Corporate Responsibility, now renamed the Center for Ethical Business Cultures. It was invented 23 years ago by CEOs driven to share their vision with a new generation of leaders. The Center for Ethical Business Cultures carries that work forward with its business partners and with two outstanding graduate schools—the University of St. Thomas Graduate School of Business and the University of Minnesota Carlson School of Management.

This is an engaging read, a thoughtful, probing effort to understand how Minnesota got to where it is today, and a thought-provoking effort to imagine what it takes to move forward.

CULTURE OF CORPORATE CITIZENSHIP

Bill Boerckel

CULTURE OF CORPORATE CITIZENSHIP

Minnesota's Business Legacy
for the Global Future

Wilfred Bockelman

Commissioned by
Minnesota Center for Corporate Responsibility

Special Note
Organizational Name Change

As this book is going to press, the Board of Directors of
the Minnesota Center for Corporate Responsibility
adopted a new name for the Center. In the future, the
Center will be known as the:

Center for Ethical Business Cultures
CEBC

2000
Galde Press, Inc.
Lakeville, Minnesota, U.S.A.

First Edition
First Printing, 2000

Library of Congress Cataloging-in-Publication Data
   Culture of corporate citizenship : Minnesota's business legacy for the
   global future / Wilfred Bockelman for the Minnesota Center for
   Corporate Responsibility.
      p.   cm.
   ISBN 1–880090–80–5 hardcover
   ISBN 1–880090–92–9 paperback
   1. Social responsibility of business—Minnesota.   2. Corporations—
Moral and ethical aspects—Minnesota.   3. Business ethics—
Minnesota.   I. Bockelman, Wilfred.   II. Minnesota Center for
Corporate Responsibility.
HD60.5.U52M63   1999
658.4'08'09776—dc21   99–38725
                                                                          CIP

Galde Press, Inc.
PO Box 460
Lakeville, Minnesota 55044–0460

CONTENTS

A description of style—*in medias res* and painting in broad strokes—
what the book is intended to do and what it is not intended to do.

Robert W. MacGregor, president emeritus
Minnesota Center for Corporate Responsibility
A brief overview of why the Minnesota Center for Corporate Responsi-
bility commissioned the publishing of this book.

Chapter 1
Is it more than a myth that Minnesota is recognized nationally and
even internationally for being in the forefront in the area of corporate
ethics, public-private partnerships and philanthropy in supporting the
arts and other activities? This opening chapter states the case that there
is substance to the myth.

Chapter 2
In medias res fashion we begin with the present. Smarting under the
moniker the *New York Times* gave to Minneapolis by referring to it as
"Murderapolis," this chapter tells the story of how local companies and
non-profits worked together to address the problem of crime.

Chapter 3
The Story of Partnerships: GMMHC, Tamarac,
A 30-year flashback. Minnesota has a history of people, corporations
and organizations working together at crucial times to solve community problems.

Chapter 4
A 96-year flashback. If this book were written in straight-line historical
fashion, from beginning to the present, this chapter might well have

been the first or at least follow an introductory chapter. When George Draper Dayton came to Minneapolis in 1902, he had no intention of starting even one store, let alone a whole chain of stores (more then 1,100 by the time of this writing).

The first one was by happenstance. But apart from that little interesting tidbit, the Dayton story gives a whole new dimension to what later would be recognized as corporate responsibility without needing the adjective "social" to give it greater respectability.

The stories of General Mills and Control Data, as described in these two chapters, are similar to that of numerous other companies in Minnesota and undoubtedly in other parts of the country.

Fast-Forward to the 1960s and the 1970s for Chapters 5 and 6. It was during these decades that the word "social" slipped in between corporate and responsibility. Milton Friedman, Nobel Prize-winning economist from the University of Chicago, didn't like the word. He insisted that the business of business is business, and that business is to make the most profit reasonably possible for company shareholders. But during the 1960s and 1970s some new thinking developed. It went under various names—enlightened self-interest, moral obligation, social consciousness.

A remarkable time, not only in Minnesota but throughout the nation. In Minnesota the ferment reached its peak in the Itasca Seminars and Spring Hill Conference in 1977. This conference served as a catalyst that resulted in the formation of two organizations still in existence at the time of this writing: the Minnesota Project on Corporate Responsibility, subsequently known as the Minnesota Center for Corporate Responsibility (MCCR), and the Minnesota Business Partnership (MBP).

Whenever the philanthropic climate of the Minnesota business culture
is discussed—even with people of distant states—almost invariably the
first reference is to the Five Percent Club.

This chapter is an interlude of a serious nature. It's a chapter for the
cynics. There will always be those who think that the very concept of
business ethics is an oxymoron. In this chapter, a retired CEO tells of
his struggles as he tried to match ethics and economics. The stories are
factual, although told anonymously, because they could easily be told
about numerous corporate executives.

There are a number of factors that have made us what we are. Even
though the answer to the question may be complex, somewhat illusive
and mostly anecdotal, it at least piques our curiosity.

An eight-page folder, *The Minnesota Principles...Toward an Ethical
Basis for Global Business,* was designed and published by the Minnesota
Center for Corporate Responsibility. These principles have been
adapted and adopted for worldwide use by the Caux Round Table, an
international organization with headquarters in Caux, Switzerland.

Another interlude of a serious kind. A review and reappraisal of where
we have been in the past and what we have learned in the present that
can be used or adapted for use in the future.

How do we adapt local experiences to meet the highly competitive
global future?

PREFACE
A WORD FROM THE AUTHOR

IN MEDIAS RES AND PAINTING IN BROAD STROKES

When you're unraveling a tangled skein of yarn or fishing line, it may be difficult to find an end with which to start. So you grab it wherever you can—maybe in the middle—and work your way forward and backward. In literary activity it's called *in medias res,* in the middle of things. My dictionary gives as an example, "Homer began his story *in medias res.*" Homer isn't a bad role model.

It is not always necessary—and at times it can be boring—to begin at the beginning and follow the calender in a straight line. So, we will begin in the middle of things, as a matter of fact, in the present. Be prepared, therefore, for some flashbacks and fast-forwards.

Admittedly this moving forward and backward can give the impression of confusion, unnecessary jumping around and just wondering where you are. A look at the table of contents will be helpful. Not only will it tell you what the chapters are about, but it will also give a rationale for their order of appearance.

An overarching thesis of the book is that there is a culture of corporate citizenship in Minnesota that has brought business, communities and non-profit agencies together in a variety of partnerships. Corporations in other parts of the world are attracted to this culture and are adopting it, or at least an adaptation of it, for themselves. For some that may sound a bit immodest, even arrogant, but let the book speak for itself.

I want to say a few words about what this book is intended to do and what it is not intended to do. I tried to paint in broad strokes, depicting some trees, as it were, but essentially highlighting the forest.

Although the book will give strong emphasis to the business community of Minnesota, particularly of Minneapolis and St. Paul, it is not essentially a history of the corporations themselves. There are three exceptions. During my research one comment I heard repeatedly from executives of other corporations was, "You simply can't underestimate the contribution of the Daytons." Hence, Chapter 4 is devoted entirely to "The Contribution of the Daytons."

Separate chapters are also devoted to two other companies, General Mills (Chapter 5) and Control Data (Chapter 6). That does not mean that they are more important than others, or that they are the only ones who gave special thought to their relationship and responsibility to the community and society as a whole. They simply illustrate what a number of other companies were beginning to do at that time.

It would be a mistake, then, to judge the importance and contributions of various corporations by counting the number of lines or paragraphs devoted to them. Two challenges confront an author: what to put in and what to leave out, and the decisions for both are equally difficult. I'm sure that once the book is in print I will wonder why in the world I left out some things that should have been there. I hope that a writer with different skills will take up the challenge of highlighting the individual trees, bushes, branches, twigs and leaves that make up the forest.

An expression much in vogue during recent decades and commonly associated with the Minnesota business culture is "corporate social responsibility." There are those who say it has become a shibboleth and needs to be addressed in a new way. Some would even say that it's redundant. By definition, corporate responsibility includes—or at least ought to include—social responsibility. Perhaps the best way to express it is with this book's title, *Culture of Corporate Citizenship.*

What would happen if we began to think of business as one of the helping professions, a term generally reserved for physicians, nurses, clergy, teachers and social workers? Wall Street has a tendency to measure corporate success by the bottom line of financial profit for stockholders, and short term at that. In the ideal world, the purpose of that profit is to serve stockholders and "stakeholders" such as customers, employees and the community and society as a whole—in other words, to help people.

Why should a book essentially about Minnesota be of interest to people outside the state? Minnesota has achieved a reputation throughout the nation and even internationally as being a leader in corporate responsibility and public-private partnerships. I would think that people and corporations in other states would be interested in what made Minnesota what it is. However, we need to guard against home-state hubris.

We know other states are being confronted with and meeting many of the same challenges that face Minnesota. For instance, I attended a meeting in St. Paul where Portland, Oregon, and Chattanooga, Tennessee, were held up as examples of creative and progressive communities. Perhaps this book could even encourage other states to share their experiences, thus benefiting all of us. We could swap our stories and learn from each other.

My special thanks to the many people, particularly the chief executive officers and other corporate staff members of Minnesota companies who gave freely of their time to enable me to have more than 50 hours of interviews. While some of them will not be mentioned in this book, I want to assure all of them that their comments provided invaluable insights to my understanding of the subject.

One problem with interviewing all these very helpful people was that most of them suggested from five to fifteen others I ought to interview. I tried to follow up on as many as I could. But then I remembered the aphorism of one of my favorite professors at Columbia University Graduate School of Journalism: "There comes a time when you gotta go with whatcha got."

However, it is difficult to decide what the cut-off point is when you "gotta go with whatcha got." The time span between the completion of the manuscript and the publication date is generally six months or more. A lot of things can happen in those six months, particularly when changes are as rapid as they are in today's business world. For instance, just before the book went to press, the Minnesota Center for Corporate Responsibility changed its name to the Center for Ethical Business Cultures.

But, if the book is also to suggest a path and challenge for the future—as this book does—then some of the events during those intervening six months are crucial and cannot be ignored. That's why a preface—what I have called "a word from the author"—is often the last to be written.

For nearly a century, Honeywell, a major Fortune 500 Company, has played a leading role as a corporate citizen in Minnesota. Before this book went to press, Honeywell was bought out by Allied Signal headquartered in New Jersey. This move came as a great surprise that has implications for the future. Fortunately, the last chapter of this book, "Where do we go from here?" is an appropriate place to deal with these implications. I am grateful to Curt Johnson, who has held many public policy positions in the state, including chief of staff to former Governor Arne Carlson, for giving an excellent evaluation of these events in the final chapter.

I am especially grateful to Robert W. MacGregor, president emeritus of the Minnesota Center for Corporate Responsibility, for commissioning me to write this book, and his assistance during the project. I also want to thank Marlys Fletcher, formerly of the MCCR staff, whose memory and files unearthed many historical documents; David Rodbourne, Terri Hastings, Robert Shoemake and Judi Olson, also from MCCR, for their critique of early drafts of the manuscript; Don Imsland, many years director of what is now MCCR, and Charles Mundale, a former MCCR staff member, for their invaluable assistance; as well as many others.

Most of my research for this book is based on anecdotal evidence. I don't apologize for that, even though I know it is held in disdain by scientific research. I know that quantifiable research is important.

The work of research and writing is time-consuming and forces many adaptations and changes of personal and family schedules. My deepest thanks to my wife, Carolyn, for her constant understanding and encouragement.

—WILFRED BOCKELMAN

PROLOGUE

Minnesota businesses have a remarkable reputation from coast to coast—and now globally—for building an envied business climate and quality of life. Minnesota and its tradition of corporate citizenship are cited frequently in business forums sponsored by the United Nations in Copenhagen, Stockholm, Istanbul, Geneva and Nairobi and at conferences in Egypt, Lebanon, Mexico, Australia, Germany, Russia, Japan and China. Indeed, Minnesota is often cited as the No. 1 location for corporate citizenship.

This book is about the Minnesota tradition of corporate citizenship. It is about business people who were—and are—proud of their accomplishments in business and in their communities. This is a story about people whose value contributed significantly to the strength and vitality of this region. It is a legacy that they wanted to pass on to the next generation of business leaders, a desire that led them to create the Minnesota Center for Corporate Responsibility in 1978. And it is a legacy that inspires other leaders around the globe. Hence the subtitle, "Minnesota's Business Legacy for the Global Future."

I am well aware that business is not held in such high regard by everybody. On a transatlantic flight to London, I sat next to a young woman en route to study theater with a grant from the Guthrie Theater in Minneapolis. I soon learned she was deeply cynical about business. She told me how greedy and selfish Twin Cities business leaders were and criticized them for not giving more money to the arts. When I mentioned seeing the long list of business contributors in the program at a recent Guthrie performance, she replied. "Oh, they just do that for selfish advertising." This bright young woman didn't even know that her scholarship was paid for by Twin Cities businesses.

On another trip, visiting with American students in a pizza parlor in Milan, I engaged in a spirited conversation about business practices. They were all studying economics. When they heard of my work in business ethics, they challenged the term as an oxymoron. They described U.S. businesses as corrupt, out to make a fast buck at public expense.

A Dayton Hudson vice president told me of a meeting he had in the 1970s at the University of Minnesota. After his speech on the values of the market system, he was taken to task by his audience. One articulate young woman chastised him for working for such a greedy, materialistic, environmentally unfriendly corporation as Dayton's. Caught off-guard, he asked her, "What are you doing with your life that is useful?" She replied that she was on her way to an environmental education camp in northern Minnesota to teach disadvantaged minority students who had never been out of the city, that she was using her talents to help these students. On hearing his story, I told the VP, "What you should have said to this young woman is that the very camp where she teaches was conceived and initiated by Dayton Hudson, who also provided the camp with major funding and paid her salary."

One very important reason for writing this book is to put the story straight, to lay out the values, the commitments and some of the accomplishments of Twin Cities business leaders in shaping the vibrant communities we live in today.

An equally important reason is a gnawing apprehension that as business has changed over the years, the commitment to corporate citizenship may be eroding.

What were once family-owned businesses became publicly held corporations and/or were acquired by larger companies from outside Minnesota. Many feared that new owners would lack the fervent commitment to corporate citizenship for which Minnesota is recognized. Today, some argue these values have indeed eroded. Others insist that there has been no change in commitment, only a different approach. Different times, they say, call for different approaches. What worked in the 1970s isn't automatically right for the 1990s.

Yet, as the generations of leadership change, the apprehension persists in some quarters. Are we in danger of losing our way?

Certainly, we cannot—should not—live in the past. Times are different today. The business demands on CEOs are more intense, more complex and coming from many parts of the globe. But there are lessons to be learned.

Philosopher George Santayana reminded us that those who don't remember the past are condemned to repeat it. Of course, that assumes the past is full of mistakes we would be wise not to repeat. But it is also important to remember past accomplishments and build on them for the future.

A few years ago MCCR assembled representatives of major Minnesota business firms to articulate a series of statements that became known as "The Minnesota Principles." That document was both a statement of the way we believe business has been and is conducted here and a statement of our aspirations for all business stakeholders. It took the lessons of the past to shape a road for the future. MCCR's document was picked up by a Swiss-based business leadership group called the Caux Round Table (CRT), which includes senior business leaders from all over the world. Transformed under MCCR's leadership, the "Minnesota Principles" are now the Caux Round Table *Principles of Business.*

In commissioning Wilfred Bockelman to tell the story of Minnesota's business culture, MCCR sought not only a more detailed chronicle of, but also a deeper understanding of "why." Why do so many business leaders in Minnesota have such strong conviction that they owe something to the community? And why and how do they factor this conviction to the financial bottom line of their corporations?

Mr. Bockelman has probed the experiences of many—though by no stretch of the imagination, all—of Minnesota's finest business leaders. He has looked into the accomplishments, and some of the failures, as our companies have struggled to address difficult social issues. He has laid out a number of tough challenges for all of us to consider. But most important, he has told the story, and told it well. For that we are in his debt.

—ROBERT W. MACGREGOR
president emeritus
Minnesota Center for Corporate Responsibility

Chapter I

WHY THIS BOOK? WHY NOW?

I heard so much about the city of Minneapolis,
about its Chamber of Commerce, about the
public spirit of its business community, about your
remarkable Five Percent Club—that I feel a bit like
Dorothy in the Land of Oz. I had to come to the
Emerald City myself to see if it really exists.
—*from a speech by John D. Rockefeller III*
to the Minneapolis Chamber of Commerce, June 30, 1977

In the interviews during the research for this book, the first question usually was quite general. "Is it your impression that there is something different and unique about Minnesota?"

The first, immediate answer that came back was usually "Yes," although often with a bit of hesitancy and some caveats. What was really meant by "different"? Different from what? Was Minnesota the only place where hard core issues were being addressed? After some discussion, clarification and modification of the question and a hesitancy for fear of being too prideful, the answer usually was still "Yes," although at times with some limitations.

The answer from Dale Olseth, president and CEO of BSI, a company that deals with surface modification sciences, was "I'd say yes, a strong yes, a strong yes! Part of it is probably the value system of the Midwest, which I think is different from the coasts. Garrison Keillor, the famous storyteller from Minnesota, once said, 'Don't let anyone tell you that values are formed on the East Coast or West Coast. While a lot of the press lives on the two coasts, the real America is in the heartland.'"

Granting that Keillor's comments may be oversimplified, Olseth nevertheless feels strongly that Minnesota and the Midwest do have a unique culture.

David Koch, chairman of the board of Graco, Inc., expressed a more qualified view. "Are we really different?" Koch asked. "There is some feeling that we are, but I'm not sure the facts would substantiate that. I think we have an inordinate number of entrepreneurs in this state. I'm not sure what the reason is. We don't have the most attractive weather nor tax climate for business. Maybe it's the vigorousness of four distinct seasons. Spring is going to come to Minnesota regardless of the fact that it's ten degrees below zero this morning."

In his position as president of the Minnesota AFL-CIO, Bernard Brommer relates to building contractors in other parts of the country. The nature of the construction industry is such that at various times contractors need more workers than are available locally. "In such cases," Brommer said, "there is always a great demand for workers from Minnesota, because they are known for their work ethic."

"I grew up in this state," said John Roe, CEO of the Bemis Company. "But then I went away to college and graduate school and work. Before I left, I don't think I was aware that there was something unusual about this city or state. After working in three other states and then coming back, I became aware for the first time that there was something different. Everybody should have the opportunity to see it from the outside in order to appreciate what we have."

In attempt to define that difference, Roe said, "There seemed to be a spirit of cooperation among many of the fundamental groups here, whether it be business and government, business and the working force, business and the arts. This had not been as noticeable in the other places where I have lived."

Dr. James Reinertsen, then CEO of Health System Minnesota, said that while he was still in private practice, following his graduation from Harvard Medical School, he was often amazed at how willingly Minnesota physicians consulted with each other in diagnosis of difficult cases. He did not find this same kind of partnership and cooperation in some other parts of the country.

In 1985, Philip Jenni, finance director of the Citizen's League, participated in making a video tape for the League entitled, *Minnesota Difference: Politics as Culture*.

"There was clearly something different here," said Jenni, "in the way the business community, particularly, engaged in public policy issues. We had some outstanding, bright people like Wheelock Whitney and Elmer Andersen, and the business community also produced people involved in that sort of thing."

"There is a lot that sets Minnesota apart from other states," said Leonard Inskip, public affairs columnist of the *Minneapolis Star Tribune*. "I could not do the job I do here in any other state, at least not as successfully. Minnesota has this unique central focus in the Twin Cities. The big foundations are here, the University of Minnesota and several colleges and universities, the seat of the state government, and a strong business community. In some other states, the capital is in one place, the university in another, and the major businesses in still another. Here in Minneapolis, I can meet face to face with the leaders in any of these areas in 15 minutes."

However, the real purpose of this book is not the issue of whether Minnesota or the Twin Cities are different from other places. After all, virtually every place is different from every other place. The real question is, what is there about this state that causes people from other parts of the United States and some foreign countries to think that there is something unique about Minnesota?

What's the evidence? Most of it, at least in this chapter, is anecdotal. That's what you get when you paint in broad strokes. Fully aware that social science research tends to discount anecdotal evidence and hold it in disdain, one might, however, ask, "How many anecdotes does it take to make a statistic?"

Four characteristics usually referred to by those who were interviewed were the state's business culture, its successful public-private partnerships, its record in philanthropy, and its flourishing arts community.

In the early years of its history the state was rich in salubrious farmland, timber and mineral deposits supporting its economy through agriculture, forestry, and mining. In recent times the state has become more dependent on a service economy, particularly the harnessing of the computer and the information age.

Business, however, is the all-encompassing activity that ties together manufacturing, marketing, exchange of commodities, research, social relations, health care, education, encouragement of the arts, and philanthropy.

Philosophers, educators, sociologists, economists, government and religious leaders may be the critics and planners of a society. People of good will may give of their wealth, but business in some form or other not only creates the wealth but also plays a leading role in determining how that wealth is to be used and in putting together the structures that will operate in a market economy.

All the more reason why these various sectors of society need to work together. And it is this culture of partnership in the Minnesota business community that has attracted national and international attention.

In 1983, New Jersey Governor Thomas Keane and 17 business leaders from New Jersey spent three days in Minnesota and interviewed 61 Minnesota business leaders.

Reporting on that visit in an article, "The Minnesota Gift," Scott McVay, executive director of the Geraldine R. Dodge Foundation, Morristown, New Jersey, wrote, "If anybody wonders if the American dream is alive and well, travel to Minnesota, for whatever you touch in that community, you will find yourself close to the soul of a place that gains and grows by giving ... the spirit of cooperation and the recognition of the fundamental interconnection of all the parts have reached a uniquely evolved form in Minnesota."

This trip, says McVay, "was the first example, to our knowledge, of a group of CEOs from one state traveling to another *strictly in the public interest.* I can't tell you how impressed we were with that experience. We went back home and organized a public-private partnership and started a Five Percent Club, which is still in existence today.

"We knew of the lakes and the cold winters. We had heard of five percent and two percent clubs (where corporations give away that percent of their profits before taxes). We knew of Dayton-Hudson, General Mills, 3M, Honeywell, Control Data, nine public radio stations, the Minneapolis *Star and Tribune,* the University of Minnesota, Carlton College, Prairie Home Companion, Citizens League, Mayo Clinic, health maintenance organizations, St. Olaf College, Tyrone Guthrie Theater, Walker Art Center, but we did not know what made them tick. Separately and together.

"We learned that the pattern of meeting, the habit of questioning, the trust and reaffirmation built into small transactions were second nature to them now. Like breathing out and breathing in. A third generation has picked up on this approach to doing business."

Twin Cities leaders are equally impressed with the contributions of the local business community. David Nasby, executive vice president of the General Mills Foundation, said it wasn't the artists who provided the initiative for the Guthrie Theater. "It was a group of local business and intellectual leaders who knew that we needed a world class theater," he said. "The business leaders knew very well if they were going to attract the brightest and the best from Wharton and Tuck and other great business schools, they would have to have some social and cultural amenities in this community; there had to be a quality of life here to convince people that they should come from southern California to this cold climate."

In the field of drama, the Twin Cities has two prestigious theaters, the Guthrie in Minneapolis and the Ordway in St. Paul, plus numerous other theater groups.

The Minnesota Symphony and the St. Paul Chamber Orchestra are internationally recognized, as many other musical groups. The community has 1,000 parks, many of them more than 10 acres in size. Minnesota Public Radio is recognized as the best in the country.

A typical weekend of offerings by the arts community in the Twin Cities includes 20 plays (in fact, more live theater than anywhere except New York and Washington, D.C.), six dance programs, three major art exhibits and 24 gallery shows.

The Minneapolis Institute of Arts is among the ten leading institutes of its kind in the nation. Other well-known galleries and museums include the Minnesota Children's Museum, the Walker Art Center, the Minnesota Museum of American Art, the History Center of the Minnesota Historical Society, the Science Museum, the Bell Museum of Natural History and the Weisman Art Museum.

Harlan Cleveland, former U.S. Ambassador to NATO, the first dean of the University of Minnesota's Humphrey Institute, and one of the founders of the Minnesota Meeting, credits the business community for coming up with the idea for the Minnesota Meeting. "We got a grant of $300,000 to start the Minnesota Meeting," Cleveland said, "and we thought we might break even in three years with 1,000 members. We reached our goal the first year. It was the business community, people like the Ken Daytons and Curt Carlsons, who got behind the project." Now in its 17th year, the Minnesota Meeting is one of the leading public forums in the country.

Kenneth Goodpaster, professor of business ethics at the University of St. Thomas, tells of his first encounter with the Minnesota business culture while he was teaching business ethics at the Harvard Business School. "I had been at Harvard no longer than a year when I got a call from the Minnesota Project on Corporate Responsibility (predecessor to the present Minnesota Center for Corporate Responsibility)," Goodpaster says. "I had not heard of them before. They invited me to speak at Spring Hill Center and be part of a day-long program on ethics.

"This is interesting, I thought. It's not organized by an academic or religious institution; it's not someone trying to convert business people to be good. It's a self-developed, self-imposed dialogue by business leaders themselves, trying to be literate about the social dimensions of their activities.

"This was very unusual to me. Being in the discipline of business ethics, I was used to business people approaching the topic of ethics with a certain respect but also some degree of reluctance. However, they were usually the ones who were *invited*. This was different. Here the business people themselves were the *inviters*. That automatically put Minnesota in a different place on my radar screen. I don't have the empirical data to say with certainty whether it is replicated elsewhere, but I have been around for a while, and I haven't seen a similar kind of intensity elsewhere."

Marjorie Kelly, founder and editor of *Business Ethics,* moved her magazine from Madison, Wisconsin, to Minneapolis in 1989. Kelly gave three reasons for her move to Minnesota.

"I was drawn to Minnesota as a center for corporate responsibility," Kelly said. "It seemed like a great place to publish a magazine on business ethics. The Minnesota Center for Corporate Responsibility was part of a whole tradition.

"The second reason was that I thought I could find here the means of support I needed. There were individuals here who would support a magazine like *Business Ethics.* In fact, I found that to be true. A number of CEOs and former CEOs did become my investors.

"The third reason was a chance to work in partnership with the University of St. Thomas, which is a very entrepreneurial university and is also building a reputation in business ethics."

But why this book at all, and why now? There is a feeling among some that the Minnesota business culture had an era of greatness—particularly in the 1970s.

Some are suggesting that the reputation Minnesota once enjoyed for being in the forefront is eroding. The argument goes like this: Many of the old-line companies were family-owned, with names like Bemis, Carlson, Dayton, Pillsbury, Cargill. As some of the once closely held companies became public, ownership was disbursed through stock purchases, mergers and acquisitions. People from outside the state were brought in as professional managers, some feared that these new business leaders might not be as committed to the community and its values as its predecessors had been, especially in its philanthropic activities.

In 1985, a professional study was commissioned by the Minnesota Project on Corporate Responsibility to assess whether the corporate leadership change in the Twin Cities had indeed impacted the community in a negative way. The study concluded that the fear was groundless.

"Certainly, there is a diversity of opinion about the critical problems facing the community and the best means of action to address them," the findings reported, "but no broad-based retreat from corporate responsibility is under way."

One relatively new CEO at the time was quite blunt. "The constant reminder that we're not as good as our forerunners will be a self-fulfilling prophecy if people aren't careful," he said. "I really resent it. We are no less committed to society than our predecessors were. But at this rate, we may not be given the chance to demonstrate it."

It's more than ten years now since that study was done. Despite its findings that there really was no lessening of commitment to corporate social responsibility for which Minnesota corporations had become known, the same charges that gave rise to the study in 1985 are being made again today.

Ken Dayton, for many years the CEO of the family-held Dayton Company, vigorously disputes the charge that corporate citizenship and corporate involvement in the community has diminished as family-owned companies have become public and brought in outsiders as CEOs. He quotes the old saying that the present is never as bad as you think it is, and the past was never as good as you were told it was.

"I feel very strongly that the managements of the publicly held companies have done every bit as good a job as the family owners and in most cases, better," says Dayton. "I think it is very important for this book to recognize—in fact, it could almost be the theme of the book—that the whole concept of corporate citizenship and corporate involvement has wonderfully survived the demise of the old families. It's no longer just a matter of noblesse oblige.

"There is a recognition that it is a part of being a corporate citizen, of belonging to the community. It also makes very good sense. We are in business to serve society, and for Dayton's, serving society meant that we have four constituencies: customers, employees, shareholders and the communities in which we operate, and we have an equal obligation to all of them."

Phil Jenni of the Citizens League and Robert MacGregor formerly of the Minnesota Center for Corporate Responsibility believe some of today's companies are not as committed to the same corporate values as was the case 20 years ago. Again, it's difficult to say how much of their belief is based on quantifiable evidence and how much is anecdotal. While the Citizens League and MCCR are still strong and viable agencies, financial support for them has diminished somewhat as increasing global competitiveness has forced companies to cut budgets.

This book is not a nostalgic longing for and a reliving of the "good old days." It's a call for a careful analysis and recognition that times and circumstances change, and as they change, different approaches are called for. No matter how successful the policies and programs of the past several decades were, they may not meet the needs of the globalized economy of today. Nevertheless we can learn from them.

In 1984 William Ouchi wrote a book entitled *The M-Form Society: How American Teamwork Can Recapture the Competitive Edge.* In it, he introduces the concept of "social memory."

Ouchi defines social memory as "the ability to remember what group has been flexible in the past and what groups have been unreasonably selfish."

In order to have force, Ouchi says, "A social memory must ... be enforced by a network of business, civic, and governmental associations ... In a mass society, the natural forces of community are absent. We must restore them, at least in some measure, and in a new way."

Ouchi devotes an entire chapter to Minnesota, chiefly Minneapolis and St. Paul, and cites the area as an excellent example of a community that understands the value of social memory. "Minnesota is different," he says.

Publishing this book may help Minnesota recover its social memory. The question of erosion asked in 1985 and again today will continue to be asked from time to time.

Our interest in the past is more than nostalgia. It has to do with legacy. The difference between the two is significant. Dictionary definitions form a good beginning for understanding. Hence, two definitions from Webster's Collegiate:

"*Nostalgia:* From Greek *nostos,* return home. Homesickness; a wistful or excessively sentimental sometimes abnormal yearning for return to ... some past period or irrecoverable condition.

"*Legacy:* Something received from an ancestor or predecessor or from the past."

It's possible to think you are talking about legacy and not recognize it as nostalgia. However, it is just as possible to deal with legacy and write it off as nostalgia, something that worked then but would never work today. The challenge is to recognize each of them for what they are.

In an address to the 1997 graduating class of the University of Minnesota's Carlson School of Management, Robert Dayton described the changes between the past and the present in graphic terms.

Drawing on his own experiences with Dayton's, he recalled how his grandfather, the founder of Dayton's, managed transactions in ledger books. The second generation used manual calculators that required pulling a crank each time you entered a sum. When Dayton himself joined the company, computers were programmed with stacks of punch cards and machines so huge and costly that companies shared computer time.

But the mind-blower illustration came when he told the graduates, "Yesterday you might have spent a few dollars for a graduation card for a classmate containing a silicon chip that plays 'Pomp and Circumstance' when you open it. It cost you less than two dollars. And after the novelty wears off, it gets thrown away—*discarding more processing power than existed in the entire world in 1950.*"

Dayton described the changes that took place in his own company, similar to what happened in a number of family-owned companies as they became public. "It used to be," he said, "that it was natural for companies to associate growth and well-being with the community."

"This was not just a Dayton family quirk," he said. "Community service was the basic principle of many area businesses, including not just Dayton-Hudson, but Honeywell and Pillsbury, General Mills and 3M, to name a few. These were some of the major corporations who formed the Five Percent Club, businesses giving back to the community five percent of their pretax profits."

They did this, Dayton said, "because it was the natural thing to do. Company patriarchs directly passed those values on to future management, not from the day they were hired, but from the day they were born."

For a time, newly public companies retained their family ownership principles, Dayton said, "but inevitably they had to change. As their operations grew more complex and geographically dispersed, they brought in professional management with new operating approaches."

Challenged by the rapid introduction of technology and accelerating globalization, corporations turned inward in the eighties and nineties. Driven to find more new talent and develop it faster, companies encouraged mobility and constantly changing career assignments. As a result, future executives had less time and motivation to develop roots in communities, because they knew they'd soon be pulling up those roots.

In this corporate meritocracy, how many ambitious young people would risk getting too involved with some local charity, when competitors for promotion were giving their evenings and weekends to the company?

Further describing the effects of change, Dayton said, "Previous generations of company leaders had to live up to the expectations of their families. Believe me, that is very different than meeting the expectations of a bunch of securities analysts!"

Dayton insists that his comments are not an indictment of today's companies, their professional managers, or their shareholders. He describes it rather as a system we've created, and from which most of us benefit.

Today's businesses require professional management, says Dayton, "but somehow, business leaders must find a way to also incorporate the older values. The reason has very little to do with the past, and everything to do with the future."

Expressing his own hopes for the future, Dayton told the Carlson School of Management graduates, "If I were you today, what kind of company would I want to work for? A company that stands for more than making a buck. A company that appreciates the interdependent interests of all its stakeholders—customers and shareholders, employees and communities. A company that makes a commitment to giving back to the community and encourages its employees to do the same."

It's more than just nostalgia, "a wistful or excessively sentimental, sometimes abnormal yearning for a return to some past period or irrecoverable past." It's a legacy passed down to us from which we can launch into the future.

Chapter 2

Minnesota HEALS
The Challenge of the Nineties

In media res fashion, we jump into the present to unravel our story. In following chapters, we'll dip into various events of the past to see how challenges in different eras were met in diverse ways.

Thanks to *The New York Times,* a new word was introduced into the Minnesota—or at least the Minneapolis—vocabulary in 1996. Because of the large number of homicides that had taken place, the *Times* suggested that Minneapolis might be called "Murderapolis." From January 1, 1994, to May 24,1997, 264 homicides occurred in Minneapolis. Quite a slap in the face for people who—even though with tongue in cheek—half believed that "Minnesota Nice" was more than a myth.

Few things do more to enhance a book's credibility than a willingness to face some unpleasant chapters in an otherwise glorious history. Carl Solberg's biography of Hubert Humphrey serves as a reminder that gangsterism and labor wars were part of Minnesota's past.

The opening of Mount Sinai Hospital in 1951 illustrates that even at that late date Jewish doctors were not given—or at least had great difficulty getting—privileges in Minneapolis hospitals.

Different, but equally difficult problems faced the Twin Cities in the 1990s. To have Minneapolis referred to in 1996 as Murderapolis served as a wake-up call. Early in 1997 a group of community, law enforcement, government officials and corporate representatives became concerned about the rise in violence across the Twin Cities.

Business leaders, including the CEOs of Honeywell, General Mills and Allina Health System, called a meeting of the governor and the two mayors of the Twin Cities, insisting that "it is time to act and turn this situation around."

Meetings were held twice a month to work toward a safer summer and safer years ahead, leading to the development of Minnesota HEALS (Hope, Education, Law and Safety). Since then, Minnesota HEALS has grown from a handful of people to dozens of government, corporate and community groups, convened to create hope and reduce violence.

It's interesting that they called Minnesota HEALS an initiative, implying that their efforts were a beginning of what would be a comprehensive and probably a long, complex program. The story of Minnesota HEALS highlights the distinctive contribution of private-public and business-government partnerships in solving community problems.

A key figure in this initiative was Michael R. Bonsignore, president and CEO of Honeywell, as well as the chairman of the Minnesota Business Partnership, which provided strong support for the initiative.

To be sure that any decisions or recommendations would be based on solid facts and research, the Minnesota Business Partnership retained Chuck Wexler, executive director of the Police Executive Research Forum (PERF) of Washington, D. C., to help analyze crime and develop appropriate preventive strategies.

PERF engaged David Kennedy and Anthony Braga of the Kennedy School of Government at Harvard to analyze homicides in Minneapolis that occurred over the three-year period, 1994 to 1997. This report, compiled and researched by Kennedy and Braga, was a compelling call to action.

The study addressed two questions: Whether there was an important connection between gangs and homicide, and the degree to which there was prior criminal involvement by both victims and perpetrators of the crimes.

The following seven key findings emerged:

1. The vast majority of both homicide victims and suspects or persons actually arrested were male and minority, especially African-American.

2. Most victims fell in the 14-35 age range, with 40 percent in the 14-24 range. While most arrestees and suspects also fell in 14-35 range, more than 60 percent were in the 14-24 range.

3. Firearms were implicated in two-thirds of these incidents.

4. Homicides were clustered tightly in a few Minneapolis neighborhoods, one of them in the area where the international headquarters of Honeywell is located.

5. More than 40 percent of the victims and nearly 75 percent of suspects and arrestees had arrest histories. For those who had been arrested at least once, victims averaged 7.5 arrests, and suspects and arrestees 7.4.

6. While gang membership in Minneapolis is relatively small—4 percent of the city's youth—nearly 45 percent of all homicides appear to be gang related.

7. Not all homicide in Minneapolis is gang homicide, so work should continue on strategies addressing non-gang violence, especially domestic and drug-related violence. However, since gang homicide is the largest single component of the city's homicide problem, addressing gang violence is an appropriate first step.

The location of these homicides was of particular interest. Homicides cluster tightly in a few Minneapolis neighborhoods. Since the international Honeywell headquarters is in one of those neighborhoods, one might ask, "Why do they stay there and expose their property and employees to the dangers of that kind of community?" A number of years ago an employee was killed in the Honeywell parking lot.

It's not that Honeywell had never thought of moving to the suburbs where dangers might be fewer, but in the early 1970s the Board of Directors decided to stay at their present location because it took seriously its commitment to the community. Even then Honeywell could have taken an attitude of "it's not our job to deal with the crime in this community; that's the job of the city's police force."

By the end of the summer in 1997, homicides in Minneapolis had dropped by half over 1996. That fact has not gone unnoticed throughout the country. Part of the reason for the drop in crime is attributed to the fact that business leaders insisted on a get-tough, no-tolerance policy of rounding up gang members and strict enforcement of probation.

Admittedly, overall crime remained largely unchanged in the Twin Cities metro area, but according to M. Patricia Hoven, Honeywell's vice president for Corporate Social Responsibility, what has changed is "the growing sense that momentum has shifted."

At the eighth annual meeting of the national Police Executive Research Forum, held in San Diego in 1997, Hoven and others from Honeywell were asked to tell the story of HEALS. They pointed out that Minnesota HEALS views itself as a forum and resource, where members share ideas, coordinate outreach programs and support initiatives that reduce crime and violence. However, the strategies focus not just on law enforcement, but also on education, jobs, health and mentoring.

Upon her return home, Hoven received phone calls from participants at the San Diego Forum asking for more information about HEALS, particularly how it was possible to get so many different groups in the city to work together.

"This may well be what makes the Twin Cities unique," said Hoven. "In some communities when there is a crime problem, community leaders and the police department work it out. Here in the Twin Cities, corporations, government and other agencies and foundations all work on the problem together in public-private partnerships. The 39 members of the Minnesota HEALS Advisory Board represent corporations, government and non-profit agencies."

Long-term programs by members of Minnesota HEALS include the following joint activities:

- Allina (a hospital and health care agency) and Honeywell teamed with Hennepin County and the city of Minneapolis to create the Phillips Neighborhood Partnership, to train people for jobs and improve neighborhood housing. St. Paul's 3M Company created a jobs program and is matching participants with coaches to help them make the transition to the working world.

- The StairStep Foundation hosted the first of several conferences in the African-American community on "Achieving the Dream." Those results are being shared to help provide some direction for initiatives to rejuvenate inner city neighborhoods.

- The City of Minneapolis expanded many of its programs such as Phatt Summer and What's Up telephone hotline. The park board extended hours for park programs. In addition, a pilot program is under way to allow non-profit organizations the opportunity to use school buildings after hours.

• The General Mills Foundation works with block clubs and community groups on Minneapolis' north side to reclaim troubled streets. It's about empowering the community to bring about positive change.

This effort is unique in its approach to communities. The focus of the Foundation's work is more than funding programs. General Mills has worked with neighborhood residents to develop community standards, negotiate a controversial new school site and collaborate with social service agencies and law enforcement representatives to address problem properties.

The Honeywell Foundation provided a small grant program to support the work of block clubs in the Phillips neighborhood.

• The Minneapolis Foundation convened community meetings to share information about the origins of crime and to discuss ways to create partnerships among communities, corporations and the police.

No wonder various organizations in the Twin Cities get frequent calls from all over the country with the question: "How is it that you get so many private, public and non-profit organizations to work together?"

However, the Minnesota HEALS project was not the first time various corporations and groups had worked together to solve a community problem. Nor was it the first time Honeywell and its now retired CEO James Renier had played a leading role in a similar cooperative effort.

In 1990 they founded the New Vistas School, a high school for teenage students who are mothers or expecting a child. Located in and maintained by Honeywell's corporate headquarters in Minneapolis, the school provides students with individualized and small group instruction, as well as health and social services, including parenting classes. It also provides child care and early childhood education for the students' children. Accommodations are available for up to 60 students and 70 infants, toddlers and preschoolers.

"The babies of students are just as important to us as the students themselves," said Renier. "We see the school as a way to help the parent, that is the student, give her child a decent start in life.

"The school was made possible only because business took the initiative. In the public sector, the political booby-traps, the public questions and budget problems alone would have taken years to resolve. But with business initiative, participants were brought together, problems were discovered, answers were found and working together we got under way."

Although the administration and instruction are under the supervision of the Minneapolis School Public School Systems, some adaptations and modifications had to be made, even in such a seemingly simple matter as the time schedule. No way is a student teenage mother taking care of her child going to be able to get to school by 7:30 or 8 A.M. Hence, the school day at the New Vistas School runs from 9:30 A.M. to 4 P.M.

More than 150 students have graduated from the school since its founding in 1990. Many graduates have gone on to post-secondary education or full-time employment.

Participating in the support of the school have been such agencies and companies as Minneapolis Public Health Department (on-site health promotion services), Hennepin County Community Services (child care funding), Minneapolis United Way (communications with community agencies), Phillips TLC (transportation), Dorsey & Whitney LLP (legal education and assistance), Honeywell and IBM (personal computers).

Renier was also the force behind Success by Six, a preschool preparatory program for children from poor homes, which is now used by United Ways across the country.

Chapter 3

THE STORY OF PARTNERSHIPS: GMMHC, TAMARAC, RIVERFRONT CURE, CORG AND SEMPAC

Flashback to the 1960s and 1970s when problems were erupting all over the place. The problems weren't really new. They had been developing for years. What was erupting was a new creativity in solving them. The chief ingredient of that creativity was partnerships, usually initiated and funded by the business community of the Twin Cities, and often identified by acronyms, such as GMMHC, CURE, CORG and SEMPAC, to name just a few.

It takes creativity even to pronounce them. Who would have thought that GMMHC, the shortened form for Greater Minneapolis Metropolitan Housing Corporation, would be pronounced "gimmick"? Providing 15,000 low-cost housing units since 1970, for which GMMHC became noted, is more than a gimmick.

GMMHC

Early in the 1970s Bruce Dayton, then CEO of the Dayton-Hudson Corporation, and Robert MacGregor, then vice president and executive director

of the Dayton Foundation, invited Charles Krusell to lunch. Krusell probably knew more about housing and pre-development assistance for housing developments than anyone else in the Twin Cities.

Dayton and MacGregor were about to offer him a job as president of
a corporation that did not yet exist. Not that Krusell needed a job. He was
already the executive director of the city's Housing and Redevelopment
Authority, which the federal government's Housing and Urban Development (HUD) had voted the outstanding renewal program in the United
States. Furthermore, Krusell was getting job offers from other parts of the
country.

To keep him in Minneapolis, Dayton and MacGregor suggested that he
be named the president of the yet unnamed but soon to become Greater
Minneapolis Metropolitan Housing Corporation (GMMHC). Included in
the job offer was the promise from Dayton to raise $1 million from the busi-
ness community to fund the program. And, as usual, Dayton Hudson was
the first to make a major contribution to that $1 million.

A new development had taken place in the late 1960s that opened the
door for the kind of public-private partnership for which the Twin Cites
have become famous.

Prior to that time all federally-funded low-income housing was also
federally owned. Those projects were about to be converted to private ownership. Federal funding would still be available, but it would be funneled
through non-profit and limited dividend private corporations.

What had made private funding for low-cost housing so difficult in the
past was the high risk and cost involved in the development before funding
would be available from government, banks, and other lending agencies.

Many low-cost housing projects lacked both the funds and the skills
necessary to form a corporation, design a plan of action, engage an architect and do all that had to be done before loans could be granted, let alone
revenue expected from rentals and mortgage payments.

Since its inception, GMMHC has invested more than $7 million, which has been leveraged into more than $800 million for affordable housing, a ratio of $117 of services for every one dollar invested. The business community continues to fund GMMHC.

That's the kind of vintage partnership for which Minnesota has become known. Creativity knows no bounds. By a humorous happenstance, Krusell discovered that by turning purchased property into a temporary parking lot in the three or so years between the time of purchase and the actual beginning of construction, an additional nine million dollars could be earned.

TAMARAC

In the late 1960s the Dayton Foundation, long noted for its contribution to the arts, decided to expand its philanthropy by addressing problems of social concern.

Summers were especially crucial. The expression, "long hot summer," had to do with more than three months on the calendar and high degrees of temperature. It was a metaphor for—among other things—youth out of school over the summer, frustrated with their lot in life, no jobs, time on their hands, and no planned outlet for their energies. The end result: race riots and burning sections of the city.

But summers also provided an opportunity and a challenge. Summer is a time for camping, and children do like camping. Fortunately, campsites are available in Minnesota. One of those sites was Tamarac, a camp in beautiful northern Minnesota. It had been used as a job core center. Buildings that had been in "moth balls" could easily be restored to use.

The Dayton Foundation capitalized on what Minnesota does best, bringing groups with special abilities together to work in partnership. James Gilbert, executive director of the Minneapolis YMCA, provided the skills for which the YMCA is noted, developing good camping programs. The city schools used the opportunity for remedial and special classes. The city's engineering department and building inspectors could share their expertise in planning the necessary renovations and arranging for transportation to and from the camp. And the private sector was willing to provide funding. The program was started in 1967 and ran through the 1970s on an annual budget of roughly $100,000. Some 1,400 inner-city youth were enrolled in the program, which resulted in the largest summer camp in the state.

In recalling the experience, Thomas Thompson, city engineer for Minneapolis at the time, attributed the success of the summer camp at Tamarac to a minimum of bureaucratic structure and hassle. "Nobody was interested in making sure that they got the credit for what was being done," Thompson said. "While we obviously acted with fiscal responsibility, there were times when we took short cuts in our accounting procedures. For instance, when I allowed the use of a city truck to haul provisions to the camp, it wasn't always accounted for in precise manner. But nobody really cared. We were all so glad that youth were being served. We were more interested in getting the job done than devoting energy to distribute either credit or blame properly."

RIVERFRONT

In mid-1971, John D. Rockefeller came to Minnesota with a message for the business community. CEOs of 14 of the Twin Cities largest corporations were brought together for a meeting with Rockefeller.

"We have this horrible thing called the Vietnam War going on," Rockefeller said, "and there is a great disconnect between the youth in America and business leadership. What can we do about it?"

The group suggested a retreat whose goal would be to agree on a useful project in which the business community and university and college students could engage in dialogue and collaborate on a program. Larry Sawyer was hired to direct such a program. Decker Anstrom, a political science major and student body president at Macalester College in St. Paul, reflecting some of the disaffection of students from the business community, brought together a group of young people. (Incidentally, as an indication of how times have changed, this is the same Decker Anstrom who some 20 years later was reported by *Business Week* magazine as one of the four highest-paid lobbyists for the communication industry.)

Describing the attempted dialogue, Sawyer says, "After shouting at each other for three or four days and confirming everyone's suspicion that there wasn't much to talk about, the two groups decided to attack one problem and do something together to solve it."

According to Sawyer, "this was an interesting period at the end of the baby boom, when you had tons of kids virtually living on the streets with a definite shortage of work."

The federal government, through its Comprehensive Youth Employment Training Act (CETA), made $40 a week available to young people enrolled in neighborhood youth corps projects. After all of the slots on their program were filled, 90 youth were left over for whom no jobs were available. They were described as definitely hard core unemployables, who now became the challenge for the newly formed coalition, the outgrowth of the the retreat. The Riverfront Project was born.

During the first summer, some 100 youth cleaned up the riverbanks along the Mississippi all the way from Anoka to St. Paul. They built bridges and paths and hauled away 35 semi-truckloads of trash, garbage and debris.

At the end of the year, Sawyer and his staff had an evaluation of the project. They concluded that for every $10,000 they could get from the business community, they could hire four staff people who could direct the activities of 100 young people.

Ten companies each committed themselves to $12,000. City officials were so impressed with the quantity and quality of the work done through the project that they asked Sawyer to work with 360 young people the second year. By the second year most of the CEOs delegated their involvement, but the participating companies continued full support of the project and assigned senior vice presidents to act in liaison capacities.

The third year, the program went from 360 youth to 1,365, but it started with a potential catastrophe. President Nixon impounded CETA funds in the country to stem the graft and kickbacks that had become prevalent. General Mills wrote a check of $100,000 to tide the project over until the government released the money.

The fourth year, nearly 1,800 youth were enrolled in the program. Not all of the projects were devoted to heavy muscle work. The Mixed Blood Theater in Minneapolis, still in existence today, grew out of the program.

"It was a unique project," says Sawyer. "It took a number of youth off the street in the summertime and paid them $40 a week. The projects would never have been possible without this full support of the business community. Its $120,000 contribution was leveraged into two and a half million dollars worth of services in kind, such as the loan of trucks and other equipment from Burlington Northern, Northern States Power and other businesses."

Rockefeller went to other cities to start similar programs and projects, but the Twin Cities seemed to be the place where it worked the best. Sawyer attributed the success to the unique public-private partnerships between the government and the business community.

The programs provided an opportunity to test the effectiveness of two types of programs, one entirely or largely funded and directed by the government and one jointly funded by the government and local business with greater control left in the hands of the local community.

The fully funded government program was considered as an income transfer, providing money to youth as an entitlement. Sawyer, on the other hand, looked on the project as an employment program. That meant youth were paid $40 for a 20-hour work week, *if they worked.*

"Every year we had this dialogue with the government," Sawyer said. "We basically took the position that if the program was to be run according to government rules, we were not going along. If they were willing to go with our rules, we'd play the game."

Sawyer and Anstrom told the youth, "You're getting paid two dollars an hour, so if you screw up and are going to be gone for four hours, it's going to cost you eight bucks, and you're not going to get it from us. The government would say, 'You can't do that.' And we would say, 'Yes we can. Just watch us.'

"We had some rules. Come to work on time. Leave on time and get paid for the hours you are here. We taught discipline. If they didn't work, they wouldn't get paid. If they broke a tool intentionally, they paid for it. They were taught to finish everything they started and to do their job well. Maybe that's what the Minnesota work ethic is all about."

The youth rose to the occasion, learned discipline and developed pride in the work they did. If you walk the Mississippi today, you will come across areas and paths that used to be city dumps, but are now incorporated in the city park system.

CURE, CORG AND SEMPAC

The three acronyms, CURE, CORG and SEMPAC, are prime examples of the way that political and business communities worked together. The interests of all three were similar. Even their memberships overlapped. Their goal was to have good government and their task was to find and then support the kind of people with integrity who would run for office.

CURE stood for Citizens United for Responsible Education. It was not surprising that the cultural upheaval of the 1960s should express itself in concern about education. Campaigns for local school board members became virtually as important as national elections.

The 1972 Minneapolis School Board election was crucial. One of the issues of the campaign centered around Minneapolis school superintendent John Davis. He was considered by most people as a capable, excellent superintendent. There was a feeling that Charles Stenvig, mayor of Minneapolis at the time, was using his influence to get Davis ousted. The business community felt it imperative to support Davis. Dayton Hudson assigned staff to orchestrate a search for good candidates in *both* parties to run for the school board.

The participation of the business community was totally free from any issues such as lower taxes or opposition to restrictive regulations that could have been interpreted as self-interest. Business was interested in the common good of the community and the education of youth.

What would happen if citizens united to find the best possible candidates regardless of political affiliation and then have them endorsed not only by both political parties, but by corporations and labor as well?

John Mason, a Democrat, and Carol Lind, a Republican, were approved by CURE as candidates for the school board. The DFL party, which met first, went along with the idea. They endorsed both John Mason and Carol Lind.

CURE had hoped for the same response from the Republicans, but they didn't quite get it. The Republicans endorsed Lind, but they couldn't bring themselves to endorse Mason. Although CURE got only half a victory, the idea was strong enough that both won in the general election.

Another seldom-achieved bipartisan stance brought together management and labor in endorsing both Democrat Mason and Republican Lind. The lesson to be learned is that it was possible in Minnesota, and if it was possible once, it could become a pattern for the future.

CORG and SEMPAC were similar. Both wanted to elect the best possible people for public office. CORG, Citizens Organized for Responsible Government, was city wide in scope. It was again largely the business community who led the search for high level candidates for both parties. Five of their candidates were elected.

SEMPAC, Southeast Minneapolis Planning and Coordinating Committee, was regional as the name implies. It was a coalition of a variety of agencies, including churches in southeast Minneapolis, concerned about good schools, safe streets and communities, adequate transportation, and police protection.

The word again is partnership. What might happen if there were a resurrection of the CORGs, CUREs and SEMPACs to assist both Republicans and Democrats in finding candidates for public office today?

Chapter 4

THE CONTRIBUTION
OF THE DAYTONS

"There is a debt which intelligence owes to ignorance; culture
and refinement to those less favored; prosperity to destitution.
We are our brother's keeper—and the reward in joy and
mental satisfaction is gratifying."
—George Draper Dayton

Sooner or later, one has to get back to the beginning. It's time for another
flashback—this time to 1902.

Sometimes it's hard to pinpoint when and how something actually
started. Usually there's a beginning before the beginning. That's particularly true of community characteristics, such as the high level of corporate
responsibility and public-private partnerships for which Minnesota has
become recognized throughout the years.

Long before the term corporate social responsibility was in vogue or
even spoken of as characteristic of Minnesota, George Draper Dayton

practiced it. Virtually by happenstance, he and his son founded a store in 1902 and named it Dayton's. By 1996, Dayton Hudson Corporation had 1,100 stores throughout the country.

Although it is not the purpose of this book to give in-depth histories of Minnesota corporations, in many ways Dayton's has become virtually synonymous with Minnesota, at least as a role model in corporate responsibility.

"You simply can't underestimate the contribution of the Daytons," says Edson Spencer, for many years the CEO of Honeywell.

For the newcomers to Minnesota as well as the younger generation born here, it might be instructive to hear some of the highlights of the Dayton story, beginning with the company's founder, George Draper Dayton. His quote at the beginning of this chapter depicts someone whose life is committed to the service of others.

True, some of his philosophy and practices—stores not open on Sunday, no advertising in Sunday papers—might seem almost quaint in today's culture. Yet today, more than 90 years later, one must marvel at the insight and business acumen of this bearded, five-foot-two giant of a man.

Deeply religious, Dayton believed firmly that "there's a divinity that shapes our lives." He paid high tribute to his parents, his "sweet tender mother with her long line of Christian ancestors; and my father, the dignified, intelligent Christian gentleman and his line of worthy ancestors."

The obligation of being "well-born," as Dayton put it in his autobiography, "imposes a great responsibility on one to pass on to his children, and their children, a name untarnished, clean and true.

"My life has not been my own choosing, but I have been fairly content with each line of activity, varied as they have been. Certainly I have striven to do my best all through the years—and I have enjoyed the game of business. And now after sixty years of intense living since leaving my father's home, I am loath to relinquish, and still am eager to do my bit and my best to make the going easier for those about me, and for those who are to fol-low. I love the thrills, the surprises, the new problems. And I strive to meet philosophically the disappointments, the losses, the tragedies. The greatest disappointment is that I haven't accomplished more for humanity, for the uplift of the race, for the betterment of the world."

In 1883 Dayton and his family moved from his New York birth-state to Worthington, Minnesota, to take over the Bank of Worthington. Look-ing for places to divide investment risks, he studied opportunities in Chicago, Kansas City, Denver, St. Paul and other cities and decided on Minneapolis. He stood on the corner of Seventh and Nicollet and counted the people who passed. After several months he recommended to the board of direc-tors of his Worthington bank that they buy property on Nicollet Avenue not below Fourth Street and not beyond Tenth.

Westminster Presbyterian Church, which had stood at the corner of Nicollet and Seventh for years, had burned, and the congregation relocated several blocks up Nicollet. Having heard that George Dayton, who was com-ing to town to look over some investment opportunities, was also a devout Presbyterian, leaders of the parish hoped that he might buy the hole in the ground where their church used to stand.

In 1901 Dayton did buy that property, as well as some additional frontage on Nicollet Avenue, and erected a six-story building. At the same time he also looked for tenants, and found two young men who wanted to start a dry goods store.

Dayton's investment company agreed to rent them part of the build-ing and furnish $50,000 in working capital, expecting to receive rent as land-lord and dividends as stock owners. But when the dry goods venture was about to go bankrupt, Dayton repurchased the stock. It had not been his lifelong ambition to build, merge, or acquire a string of department stores throughout the country. It wasn't his goal to open even one store.

Laconically he describes this happenstance. Suddenly, he writes, "Son Draper, who had graduated from Princeton in June 1902, and I had a store on our hands. It was very risky, but really there was nothing for us to do but go ahead with the store. We lost money, but we gained experience. I kept track of losses until they passed $100,000. Then I said, 'I don't want to know the loss. We are going to make this win.' and the result speaks for itself. It was hard to 'tear up' at Worthington and move away, but it seemed necessary."

It was typical of his self-effacing attitude not to take personal credit for the many contributions he did make to society. In 1932 Dayton gave the Baccalaureate address at Macalester College in St. Paul, Minnesota. He entitled it, "Success by Contribution Instead of Success by Acquisition." The following excerpt from the first paragraph of that address reflects his general philosophy:

> Success by contribution instead of success by acquisition. There is that [which] scattereth and yet increases. Addition by subtraction. Anomalies of speech, are they? To the unthinking, yes. But let you and me study a bit together and see if we can unravel the mysteries of history and penetrate the recesses of divine mathematics as with reverence we peer into fathomless depth of that wisdom which planned the universe and formulated the laws that have kept the worlds on their way so successfully through the centuries.

To recapitulate, for Dayton the true measure of success was not acquisition but contribution to society. There were those in the business world who had difficulty with this concept. At one time after he made a contribution of $100,000 to Macalester College, a banker refused to give him a business loan, even though he had established a successful business and had an excellent credit rating. In the banker's opinion, anyone who would give away this much money "recklessly" would be a poor credit risk.

The stories of Dayton's devotion to the application of religious principles, as he understood them, to the running of his business are legend.

Section I in the By-Laws of the Dry Goods Company, predecessor to what later became Dayton's, reads: "The incorporators of said Dry Goods Company, having unanimously agreed that there shall never be any Sunday advertising by or in behalf of said company, said agreement and decision are hereby made and declared to be binding upon all the directors, officers and agents of said Dry Goods Co."

In his autobiography thirty years later, Dayton writes:

> We have never allowed any Sunday advertising, and no inventory, repair or alteration work on Sunday. We request our buyers not to travel on the Sabbath, saying to them frankly we desire only six days' service. We really go further than the above for we say to our people occasionally that we believe the Sabbath is fundamental to the perpetuity of our nation and it is important every citizen do his part in preserving the Sabbath.

One wonders what George Draper Dayton would think if he were here today. Several of his grandsons say that while he might long for "the good old days" and not feel totally comfortable with seven-day-a-week business practices, he was also enough of a realist to accept some of the changes that the five grandsons had to make when they ran the company.

Grandson Kenneth Dayton points out, "I think it's worth noting that the change in the corporation's bylaws [to allow store openings on Sunday] was made by the second generation of Daytons. Our father, G. Nelson Dayton, before he retired from the business, knew that someday conditions would dictate doing business on Sunday. Although that did not happen in his lifetime, he wanted to make it possible for the next generation to do it when appropriate."

In response to the accusation that Dayton was anti-semitic, Bruce Dayton, who is writing a book about his grandfather, says, "I find absolutely no evidence of intolerance on my grandfather's part. In fact the evidence is overwhelmingly to the contrary, starting in his youth and continuing throughout his life. In his autobiography he writes, 'I have nothing to say as to your being Catholic, Jew, Methodist, Baptist, or something else—but I do say the most important thing anyone can do in this world is to give himself to God in loving service.'"

The late Donald Dayton, quoted in an interview in *Corporate Report of Minnesota* in January 1979, said, "I don't think Catholics or Jews were consciously excluded from the company, but I'm not saying that there would ever have been a Jewish president of Dayton's in my grandfather's time. I know of cases where we purposely and directly went out to correct that kind of situation, knowing that, maybe, we were on the shy side here or there."

The Daytons today undoubtedly would not express their religious beliefs in the same way their grandfather did. They are nonetheless as deeply committed to religious values as their grandfather was, particularly in the conviction that because they have been blessed, they owe a debt to society. They give evidence of this conviction by their many contributions, particularly to the arts. and their involvement in civic activities.

Their grandfather expressed the importance of contributions to society in this way: "There is a debt which intelligence owes to ignorance; culture and refinement to those less favored; prosperity to destitution. We are our brother's keeper—and the reward in joy and mental satisfaction is gratifying." That was not only his philosophy; he ran his business that way. And that philosophy continued in the second and third generation of Daytons.

David Draper Dayton, who went by the name of Draper, opened the first Dayton's store with his father in 1902. Later, another son, George Nelson Dayton, known as Nelson, joined the company. Draper died in 1923 at the age of 43, and Nelson took over the reins. During the late 1940s, he ceased being active in the store because of cancer and died in 1950.

During Nelson's 27 years as head of the company, he and his associates built it into one of the great stores of America. Only Hudson's in Detroit (later acquired by Dayton's), F & R Lazarus in Columbus, and Rich's in Atlanta had a comparable share of the market. In addition to running a great store, he continued his father's philanthropic program, and Dayton's became the major donor to most philanthropic drives. Dayton's was usually one of the first to be solicited and often the first to commit, thus setting the pace for the corporate community.

THE THIRD GENERATION OF DAYTONS

Nelson's five sons—Donald, Bruce, Wallace, Kenneth and Douglas—inherited the business, each of them owning 20 percent. They had joined the business after completing college and serving in World War II.

When Donald, the oldest of the five, joined the company in 1937, the store had a revenue of $17 million. He began as a stock boy after graduation from Yale. Because he had polio as a child, he was the only one of the five who did not serve in World War II.

Two other members of the Dayton family—George Dayton, a cousin of the five brothers; and two sons of Donald— Edward and Robert—had various positions of leadership, but it was the third generation of five grandsons of the founder who made all the decisions, often succeeding each other as president or vice president.

Donald was president for a while, then Bruce, and in 1970 Ken took over. Bruce simply said, "I realized Ken was a better executive, one who could do a more effective job building the organization than I could. We had been very comfortable working together. The only difference was that we used to meet in my office, but, afterwards, we met across the hall in his.

It didn't really change anything, but at the same time, we were always clear who was in charge."

Soon after their father died, the five sons got together to plan their future. They concluded that since national department store chains were buying up independent regional stores all throughout the country, their future as a family-owned store "wasn't very bright," according to Ken.

They could have sold out, and, as Donald said, "pay all of us enough to live comfortably," but that didn't appeal to them. Also, it would have been difficult for them to increase their share of the market in their one Minneapolis store. So, as Ken said, "Building a bigger and better pie would be more productive than trying to increase what was already as large a market-share as any department store in the country had."

Not only did the third generation of five Dayton brothers inherit a business with huge financial potential—it would gross $25 billion in 1996—their grandfather also left them another legacy.

Bruce describes it this way: "When our grandfather and other entrepreneurs came to Minnesota from New England and New York, they brought with them some capital and their Calvinist conscience. It was always impressed on us that we owed a debt to society as a whole and to our community in particular."

Ken's analysis was this: "I believe that the only reason for the existence of the free enterprise system is to serve society. I believe that every business must define for itself how it will serve society."

In the case of the Daytons, they were already early supporters of the stakeholder concept, the idea that corporations owe as much attention to customers, employees, and the community in which they operate as they do to the stockholders. It was a virtual obsession with them that they serve the community.

"We believe that there is no conflict between any of these constituencies or stakeholders," said Ken. "Furthermore, we believe the common denominator of all four is maximum long-range profit, without which none can be served well.

"We believe that only when we clearly recognize that we are in business to serve society rather than just to make money, only when business allies itself with the public interest, will it begin to secure its own future. In short, I believe that serving society is very much in our own enlightened self-interest and is the only way to assure our survival. Profit is our reward for serving society well."

As early as 1918, George Draper Dayton incorporated the Dayton Foundation. Actually, he said, "it was started in 1909 when my wife and I set apart $500,000, to which amount we added as we could through the years, believing it wiser to distribute through the Foundation rather than leave any large amount to be divided or distributed by will."

In 1946 Dayton's became the second corporation in the United States to give five percent of its pretax profits through its Foundation for charitable and benevolent causes, the first being S&H Green Stamps.

THE CONTRIBUTIONS OF WAYNE THOMPSON

At least a half dozen business and civic leaders told me, "You've got to talk to Wayne Thompson." Four of them also said, "The days of Wayne Thompson are over."

Who is Wayne Thompson and what is there about his work that is "over"? Thompson was brought to Minneapolis in 1965 by Donald Dayton with the support of his brothers, and for the next 16 years he was responsible for "everything outside the walls of the business" that related to Dayton's.

That task had become the special assignment of Don Dayton, who together with Booz, Allen & Hamilton consultants found Wayne Thompson and brought him to Minneapolis. Thompson was at that time the city manager of Oakland, California, the youngest person in the country ever to hold such a position.

His assignment at Dayton's was to be head of the Department of Environmental Development. "It was unique," said Ray Hoewing, vice president of the Washington-based Public Affairs Council. "No other public-affairs officer had so large a role beyond the government aspects of his company's business into the affairs of the community."

"When I came to Minneapolis," Thompson said, "Don took me to a window in the top floor of the store. 'You see all that crud down there in that slum area ?' Don said. 'It's your job to clean that up.'"

This was vintage Dayton philosophy, and Wayne Thompson was the right man to put it into practice. In addition to his own native ability, he had three things in his favor—the financial resources of the Dayton Foundation, the company's continued commitment to give five percent of its pre-tax profits to the foundation, and the personal and recognized commitment of the Daytons to a variety of causes for the betterment of the community, which could easily be leveraged into getting similar support from other corporations and organizations.

Ken Dayton made it a practice to take new CEOs in the community out for lunch and brief them on the expectations of Minnesota business culture. Ken would usually open the conversation with comments like this: "I'm glad you've come to the Twin Cities. The corporation that hired you knew what it was doing. It's a good company, and you're the right person for the job. And now let me tell you a little about what the community expects of it's CEOs.

"I happen to think, he said, "that being the CEO of a corporation, large or small, is every bit as high a calling as being an educator, or being in the field of religion, medicine, law or any other occupation. The CEO has the opportunity to impact a community more than almost anyone else, and therefore it is an incredibly high calling and opportunity to make this community and this nation a better place."

Thompson's method of operation during his 16 years at Dayton's was described by Ted Kolderie in a September 1981 issue of *Corporate Report* under the title, "The Power of Quiet Influence." Kolderie wrote, "Thompson was the most influential corporate public-affairs officer in the area, but always managed to stay behind the scenes. He was always pushing civic projects, but always through others, and always out of view."

Although much of what Thompson did grew from ideas of Donald, Bruce, and Kenneth Dayton, says Kolderie, "many of the ideas were Wayne's own."

"One of Wayne's most important achievements was the establishment of the Five Percent Club, later called the Minnesota Keystone Program^{SM}," said Bruce Dayton. "I believe both of those were instrumental in encouraging local corporations to enhance their charitable giving and in making Minneapolis a national example."

"If there is any change," said Ken Dayton in a recent interview, "I think the era of Wayne Thompson is over. Today's CEOs can't be on all community boards. They can't have everyone in the community run to them. They just aren't that available. Every corporation should have someone of real stature, who does more than just dispense funds. They should have a professional devoting full time to building the communities in which they operate."

Thompson had the ability to bring together leaders from the corporate and civic world both to identify and to solve metropolitan problems. Dayton-Hudson hired an excellent staff of knowledgeable executives with political and civic experience.

Thompson was a key player in the development of housing programs, in renewal of the lower loop from (4th Street down to the river) and the upper loop (from 8th street up on Nicollet Avenue), in the building of the Metrodome, and in the development of Nicollet Mall and the skyway system.

It would be difficult to find any major civic development between 1965 and 1981 that did not somehow have the imprint of Wayne Thompson on it. In his constant work behind the scenes described by Kolderie as "the power of quiet influence," he was a catalyst who could get corporations to join efforts in vitalizing the community. He was particularly successful in bringing banks aboard in financial support of major community projects.

According to John Cowles Jr., editor of the *Minneapolis Tribune* at the time, until then banks had not given strong financial support to individual community projects. What relatively small contributions they did make, they made through the bank clearing house system. Cowles and Thompson got them to think in bigger terms. After all, Dayton's and other major corporations had their deposits in the banks, and they felt virtually compelled to participate in civic projects.

Dayton's and Thompson set the pattern that brought the banks in as a major player in putting both money and personnel into community development. Jim Hetland, an earlier director of the Citizen's League, and later chairman of the Metropolitan Council, joined the staff of First Bank as director of public affairs. He directed his assistants, first Todd Otis, and later Michael LaBrosse to study and report on the major needs of the community so that corporations could have a clearer picture of what the needs were. The question was shifted from how can we keep on doing what we have been doing to how should we allocate our resources to do what needs to be done?

But even then, times were beginning to change, a change that caused some to speculate that "the days of Wayne Thompson are over." Some people were beginning to question whether the model set by Dayton's would continue.

Kolderie predicted in 1981 that the ethic of civic involvement by Twin Cities area business would change. "It will change, but it will hold," Kolderie said.

"A large part of the strength and continuity of future corporate involvement in the Twin Cities," said Kolderie, "will come from that cadre of public-affairs officers who function as much to represent the community to the company as the company to the community."

What the community needs, Ken Dayton said, "is not a professional who just dispenses funds, but a professional devoting full time to building the communities in which we operate."

None of the five third-generation Dayton brothers are presently an official part of the board or executive staff of The Dayton Hudson Corporation. The company went public in 1967. Don died in 1989. Bruce left in 1977. Ken retired in 1983, the last of the family to have a connection with the corporation. Wallace and Douglas left to follow other interests, largely committed to environmental concerns.

Dayton-Hudson serves as an example of what loyalty to the community can do. There is a feeling among some that global competition today is so intense that CEOs simply can't devote time to maintaining good community relations.

"I can understand that feeling," says Verne Johnson, former vice president for planning at General Mills, "but I wouldn't want to let people off the hook for thinking that way. We would not have a Dayton's in Minneapolis today, and all that they continue to bring to this community, if they had not been such a responsible corporate citizen that when they almost became victims of a hostile take-over twelve years ago that the whole community rose up, and the governor called a special session of the legislature to pass a law that would keep that from happening."

Chapter 5

NOT ONLY WHAT PEOPLE EAT FOR BREAKFAST, BUT ALSO WHERE AND HOW THEY LIVE

As the name suggests, General Mills is a milling company. Its origins go back to the late 1800s and early 1900s. One of its chief products is breakfast cereals. At various times it has experimented with a variety of products, mostly related to foods and restaurants, but also others as seemingly disparate as apparel, toys and games, and speciality retailing. During recent years it has sold off most of its non-food-related divisions and has focused on packaged foods.

As of mid-1996, it ranked 156th among Fortune 500 companies, and the fifth largest public company in Minnesota, with its international headquarters in Minneapolis.

Stevens Court sounds like a street address, more likely a residential area. How are General Mills and Stevens Court related?

Verne Johnson, for many years the vice president for corporate planning at General Mills, had long felt that today's corporations owe something to the community in which they are located, not only as a philanthropic venture but as a part of its ongoing business enterprise.

"I believe that a company that attempts to improve its city and its society is entitled to a profit," Johnson said. "We have to lay the idea to rest that social responsibility is incompatible with profit. We have to begin seeking out new areas of activity where both goals can be met and where there is a happy confluence of profit and principle."

James Summer, president of General Mills during the 1970s, said, "You start with the assumption that a corporation should be a good citizen and contribute to less fortunate parts of the community. Top management at General Mills wanted to make an impact more far-reaching than the usual exercise of social responsibility in the non-profit world…and in a way we didn't see government and other agencies or other corporations doing. Instead we wanted to take on projects, helping manage and finance them through the involvement of both staff officers and operating employees. Another objective was to also get a small return on our capital investment— or at least to break even."

One area of activity that attracted General Mills was Stevens Court, a 50-block area just south of the Minneapolis business district.

General Mills announced in 1973 that it would participate in a Stevens Court housing project. A new corporation, Stevens Court, Inc., was formed to renovate, lease, and manage 300 living units to house approximately 1,000 residents. General Mills would retain a 51 percent interest (later increased to 65 percent) and would make additional financial commitments of about half a million dollars over the next 12 to 18 months.

The goals of the project were to stabilize and preserve the character of the neighborhood, to renovate and not replace and to provide good, low-middle income housing which would produce a profit on their investment— perhaps a lower than maximum profit, but still a profit.

Not-for-profit organizations and the government are still looked to as the major force for solving community social problems. However, non-profits often lack sufficient funds for continued support of projects. Sometimes they also are short on the business skills needed to find solutions. So in addition to providing funds, General Mills leadership also became involved in guiding the project through various stages. It applied business discipline to community services.

In 1982 the housing project was sold to the March Company in Boston, and General Mills recovered its investment of $7 million, ready to put it to use for another project.

It was understood from the start that General Mills was not joining in this project to fulfill its social responsibility through traditional philanthropy but through sound business procedures. General Mills defines this activity as corporate social investment. Although it could undoubtedly have gotten better immediate financial returns by investing elsewhere, its participation in the Stevens Court project brought useful returns of another kind.

There was the good will of the immediate community as well as good public relations nationally when the success of this experimental venture was reported in the media. Furthermore, the top level executives insist that as a result of being involved in the project, their own executive skills were improved. They worked with a group of people quite different from their usual experience and they came to a better understanding of how to deal with people and social problems.

Stephen Rothschild, a former executive vice president of General Mills, said that the fact that General Mills allowed him and others to work on special projects "made us better managers, prouder to be part of General Mills, and contributed to creating a better place. Our visions were broader as a result, and we were out in the community meeting different people and getting stimulated with different ideas. We were closer to the real world in some ways. It was something that was important for our lives. Selling cereal is not what everybody wants to do all the time; I didn't and so it was important that I find some balance, and this was a way to do that."

ALTCARE

As a result of its favorable experience with Stevens Court, General Mills was ready to take on another experiment. It established two criteria for selecting a new project. First, General Mills executives would have to be actively involved. As one of the executives said, "We learned that you can't put anything less into a social responsibility project than you put into marketing new products. You've got to send in your first team."

The second criteria was that the project would have to be designed to return a profit to General Mills. That did not mean that every aspect of the project had to produce a profit, but if some areas showed a loss, another project would have to make up for that loss.

And there would be some losses. The general philosophy was that if *everything* worked, they weren't taking enough risks. As one person said, "If we decided to work only with people who are sure fire winners, we wouldn't be doing anything original. A bank can do that."

General Mills worked in cooperation with the Wilder Foundation. The goal for a new experimental project was to revolutionize the way America provides health care for its elderly.

Two corporations were formed, Altcare Development and The Altcare Capital Corporation. General Mills and Wilder each committed $300,000 to the first corporation. Its goal was to get the federal and state governments to provide economic incentives to health care providers to design programs that could be used by the elderly who wanted to continue living in their own homes.

The second company, The Altcare Capital Corporation, would provide capital in the form of below-market-loans to service providers to encourage them to develop new approaches to the delivery of services for the elderly. The corporation would use $5.3 million from Wilder and General Mills and about an equal amount in government loans. As one General Mills vice president put it, "the government sector, the private sector and the not-for-profit sector can cooperate as one sector."

ELDER HOMESTEAD

General Mills, the Wilder Foundation and the Housing Alliance, a corporation formed by Minneapolis architect Arvid Elness and Williams Financial Services, cooperated to build Elder Homestead, a 30-unit complex. It was designed for older persons who cannot or choose not to remain in their present living arrangements, and who require or want 24-hour non-medical supervision and access to a full range of coordinated health and social services. The residents pay a monthly program fee to cover the costs of these services as they are needed.

The chief characteristic of this arrangement is the "unbundling" of services so that the building and program are designed to adapt to the individuals rather than forcing all residents to adapt to the building and programs, some of which they may not need. The whole financial key is the separation of the housing from the health care services, unlike traditional nursing homes which combine these two elements. In 1996, nine years after opening, fees remained highly competitive and lower than skilled nursing care.

In 1994 the Altcare Corporation sold its 30-unit innovative program to VOA Health Services, a Twin Cities division of Louisiana-based Volunteers of America. VOA announced an ambitious expansion project for the Elder Homestead concept that, if followed through, could represent an investment of more than $12 million.

The Elder Homestead experiment has become a model for more than 100 facilities built throughout the country during the past nine years. In 1987 General Mills received the prestigious Dively Award from Harvard

Business School, given to one American corporation each year for an out-standing contribution to community betterment.

SIYEZA, ITALIAN ACCENT AND GLORY FOODS

One could begin to wonder whether General Mills is so excited about its Stevens Court, Altcare and Elder Homestead projects that it might forget its chief business is processing grains for table use.

Or could it be that it is precisely this kind of business activity that has given Minnesota companies the reputation of corporate responsibility? To live up to this reputation, the corporations must first of all discipline them-selves to be profitable, to honor their commitments to customers, employ-ees and stockholders. They then have the choice as to how far they want to go extra-curricular fashion—even dream—to tackle the massive problems of society.

General Mills and other Minnesota corporations have taken that extra step. With Stevens Court, Altcare and Elder Homestead under its belt, Gen-eral Mills explored several other projects. After rejecting one that would have been similar to its other projects, it settled on Siyeza. The Siyeza story illustrates the challenges and frustrations encountered on the path from dreams to realities.

In 1995 Ted Cushmore, a General Mills executive pondering retirement, attended a breakfast honoring Dr. Martin Luther King Jr. The speaker, Harry Belafonte, challenged the group to move from ideas to action. Cushmore was impressed. He went to the General Mills Foundation to see how he might answer the challenge to turn dreams into reality.

The Foundation referred Cushmore to Alfred Babington-Johnson, founder of the Stairstep Foundation, who in turn referred him to Beck Hor-ton, an African-American entrepreneur running a frozen foods contract plant in North Minneapolis. Horton had an idea for a job-creating venture that went under the name of Italian Accent. General Mills was intrigued by Italian Accent and committed $1 million as a corporate social investment.

And then it hit a snag. Italian Accent lost its major customer, was unable to replace the business and had to discontinue operations in three months. When Stephen Sanger, CEO of General Mills, was told about this, he said, "You know when this happens to minority entrepreneurs, it's usually the end of the story. Well, this isn't going to be the end of the story." General Mills reaffirmed its commitment and urged Cushmore and Babington-Johnson to look for an alternative.

Meanwhile Babington-Johnson visited his mother in Tennessee and marveled at her traditional southern cooking. She took him to a local Kroger store to show him the fabulous products of Glory Foods.

Babington-Johnson got in touch with Bill Williams, a Columbus, Ohio, entrepreneur, founder of Glory Foods. They discussed the possibility of Glory Foods becoming involved in a project succeeding Italian Accent in Minneapolis.

Three General Mills executives flew to Columbus with Babington-Johnson to meet Williams and then on to South Carolina to tour Glory Foods production facilities.

Williams explored the opportunity of "frozen home replacement meals" that would be produced in the former Italian Accent plant in Minneapolis. General Mills helped research and analyze the idea's potential, and also increased its commitment to $1.5 million in the form of a loan with no interest and no term.

At the same time Glory Foods invested $50,000 while Stairstep invested $100,000, raised from African-Americans in the form of equity. Thus Glory Foods has one-third ownership and Stairstep has two-thirds ownership in the venture. As the company reaches financial benchmarks, one-third ownership will transfer to its primarily African-American employees. US Bancorp chairman and CEO Jack Grundhofer embraced the concept and committed $1.2 million in operating financing and to purchase stock in the venture. The new venture is called Siyeza, inspired by a stirring African song sung by a 110-voice African-American community choir.

In 1998 a ribbon-cutting ceremony launched the new Siyeza plant employing some fifty area residents from the inner city, with the expectation to employ 150 within twelve months.

That's vintage Minnesota creative partnership.

Chapter 6

A COMPULSION TO GO NORTH WHEN EVERYBODY IS GOING SOUTH

Early in 1967 William C. Norris, founder and CEO of Control Data Corporation, attended a seminar for chief executive officers, led by Whitney Young, head of the National Urban League.

It couldn't have come at a more appropriate time. The savage destruction and race riots throughout the nation caused July of that year to be described as the beginning of "a long hot summer." In other parts of the country, yes. But in Minnesota? Surely not. Couldn't be. After all, wasn't this the state that prided itself on a high level of civility? Nevertheless, race riots broke out in Minneapolis and buildings on Plymouth Avenue were in flames.

Remembering how impressed he had been with the presentations of Whitney Young earlier in the year, Bill Norris flew to New York to get Young's advice. His question was, "What can a company like Control Data do to help avoid a repetition of this kind of disaster?"

Young had a simple answer: "Jobs. Until these young blacks have jobs, until they have something to look forward to and work for, you're going to have trouble in Minneapolis and everywhere else."

Could this mean that workers were not just a means to an end that would reflect itself in a profitable bottom line? Might it mean that *corporations* could be a means to an end, providing jobs for workers, and thus avoiding future burning of cities? Norris expressed it in his usual crusty style when he got back home. "My God, you can't do business in a society that's burning." Keeping society from burning and running a successful company were interdependent, and it seemed virtually impossible to give a higher priority to one than to the other.

Norbert Berg, a close associate of Norris, describes the experience as "Norris's Road to Damascus," a reference to the Apostle Paul's life-changing experience on the way to Damascus.

"I'm not sure Bill was as much aware of it as I was, watching from the side," Berg said, "but he was different. It was like he'd had his eyes opened. He had become aware of problems and of his ability to do something about them. I always believed Whitney Young did that."

The first thing Norris did when he got back from New York was to call his staff together and insist that as a major employer, Control Data had an obligation to start hiring African-Americans in significant number "not as an obligation, but as a business necessity."

The commitment to hiring African-Americans was nothing new for Control Data. It had followed a policy of non-discrimination in employment since its beginning, but very few minorities had been actually hired.

"We thought we had done our job when we placed employment ads in the paper," Berg said. "After all, we have a nice place out here in the suburbs, and everybody would obviously be glad to work here if they just knew jobs were available. That shows how out of touch we were with reality, even with the best of intentions on our part."

The reality was that the people who needed jobs lived closer to the inner city and would find it difficult to come all the way to our office in the suburbs. That meant that if we were really serious in wanting to hire African-Americans in large numbers, Berg said, "we would have to build a factory where they lived rather than expect them come to where our factory or office was."

Norris made some other demands for what came to be known as The Northside Plant. First of all, it meant putting the plant in the middle of the inner city. But he called in the people who lived there to help decide if they wanted a factory there and where it should be. Charles Stenvig, then mayor of Minneapolis, complained that while the people in the community were involved in the planning, he did not find out about it until he read it in the paper.

Norris wanted the community to know that Control Data "was serious in its intentions and had come to stay." It would be a new building, so attractive "that people would take pride in it and protect it from vandalism, which they would not be likely to do for an old beat-up structure."

But there was something even more daring and risky about Norris's commitment. Prudence might have dictated at most to begin this venture with a product requiring mostly low-skilled workers, one not too vital to the business so that if the project failed or the input was not up to standard, the shortfall would not be critical.

Norris insisted that the new factory should produce a recognizable product, something that the people could see as contributing to the company's business, something they could associate with and take pride in, something that would "require enough skill to provide motivation for learning and a realistic basis for career progress—a future."

Maybe it was that stubborn attitude that influenced James C. Worthy to choose a Norris quotation for the flyleaf just before the title page in his book, *William C. Norris—Portrait of a Maverick:* "Whenever I see every-body going south, I have a great compulsion to go north."

Bill Norris stretched the point of "going north" even farther. He made the worldwide production of Control Data dependent on the output of this plant. Worthy points out that the feelings of the manufacturing staff "were ambivalent, not to say schizophrenic…Some felt, 'My God, this is a dumb idea. We'll never be able to make it work.'"

Worthy continues, "But it had to work—or else. This was precisely what Norris intended. As his associates had long since learned, he dislikes start-ing anything on a trial basis. To do something on trial is to admit in advance the possibility of failure, "and if you leave room for failure, he will tell you, 'you're very likely to fail.' He was determined not to run any such chance with this new venture. He knew there would be difficulties, and he delib-erately created a situation that left no room for retreat."

But perhaps even Norris did not realize how difficult—even bizarre—some of the problems might be, such as the abnormally high rate of absen-teeism on Mondays. Why Mondays?

The lifestyles in the community often helped explain why workers landed in jail on week-ends. The solution seemed equally bizarre. An attorney worked out an arrangement with the court and the police that allowed Gary Lohn, later to become a Control Data vice president, to visit the city jail on Monday morning and bail out any company employees who had run afoul of the law.

Worthy writes that "the procedure became so routine that the court authorized Control Data to print its own bail bond forms, complete with company logo; Lohn's signature was sufficient to obtain the employee's release—in effect— into Control Data's custody."

That the need for this form of special assistance gradually faded cor-roborated Norris's conviction that if you give people responsibility, sup-port them and nurture them along in growth, they will rise to the occasion.

A new employee had to fail three times before he was dropped. After the first failure, an effort was made to determine the cause and to assign the individual to a job better suited to his or her capabilities. A similar procedure was followed after a second failure. This procedure worked so well that remarkably few people failed entirely. Unskilled and untried people were given a chance to succeed and most of them did.

Worthy reports in his book, published in 1987, that "in the nearly twenty years the plant has been in operation, many of those who originally brought no or few job skills to the workplace have advanced to skilled ranks and some into supervision and management: eventually, virtually the entire original staff of managers, foremen, and lead persons were replaced by people brought up from the ranks of the Northside plant itself."

Norris made it plain to everybody that this project was not a philanthropic venture, one that could live only as long as it received continuing grants from foundations or other organizations. It had to meet the strict business bottom line of becoming profitable or it would be discontinued. He adamantly insisted in regard to the venture that "if all it does is make jobs that keep people busy and give them some income, it doesn't prove anything. *It has to be a business success before it can be a social success.*"

Since one of the main goals of the project was to provide jobs for people in the community, and since a large number of those who came to work were single mothers, childcare became an immediate issue. Control Data planned a childcare center right in the building, so that parents could leave children where they worked. But again, people in the community were involved in deciding what kind of center would be most helpful. Since some companies in the immediate area were not able to have a day care center of their own, the typical Minnesota concept of collaboration and partnering provided assistance. Major downtown companies like Dayton Hudson, Northwestern Bell and others joined Control Data in taking slots, thus servicing five employers by providing childcare service.

Control Data was ready to take on another project. One day Berg said to Norris, "You know, we could staff an entire factory or office with part-time workers. Mothers would have an easier time working if they could be home in the afternoon when their children come home from school. Others would be free to work in the late afternoon and early into the evening. We could even put in a third shift and work the plant twelve hours a day."

Norris had a brief reply, "That's a good idea. You ought to do that." And another project was started, this one in the Selby-Dale area of St. Paul. One factor was lacking that had made the Northside project so successful. The first plant had a built-in customer, Control Data itself, which needed the computer parts and peripheral equipment manufactured at the Northside plant.

By the time plans were made for the Selby-Dale plant, the computer industry itself was undergoing a recession, and Control Data had no need for another assembly line. However, since it produced numerous publications, instructional manuals and catalogues, the Selby-Dale project became a bindery that served not only Control Data's needs, but was also able to do bindery work for other companies.

The Selby-Dale section of St. Paul was an area of high unemployment where no new industrial job-producing investment had been made since before the turn of the century. Within five years it employed 450 people, all of them working part-time, mothers while the kids were at school and the kids themselves after they got home from school.

Worthy reports that "as with the Northside Minneapolis plant, the Selby-Dale facility was the pride of both the company and the community. A dozen years after the new facility was opened, its attractive exterior had not been marred by a single line of graffiti—this in a neighborhood where graffiti is common. No burglar alarm was ever found necessary."

Norris had other projects in mind in other parts of the country, in Washington, D. C., Toledo, Ohio, and San Antonio, Texas, all operating on the principle of private industry working together with government and a variety of grants.

The projects all had one thing in common: they were to become self-sufficient and turn a profit. Where Norris ran into problems was the length of time it took for some of them to become profitable, and some never did. He had a continuing run-in with Wall Street, which was always more interested in short-term, next-quarter profits. Some of his own staff also were critical.

"Nothing about Control Data Corporation has attracted as much attention," writes Worthy, "as its policy of addressing unmet society needs as profitable business opportunities. It is this policy that is largely responsible for the frequency with which Norris is described as quixotic, visionary, and impractical. And why he is blamed by many for the serious difficulties in which the company found itself in 1985. Yet it is also this policy that most firmly cements the positions of William C. Norris and Control Data Corporation in the economic and social history of our time."

Today Control Data no longer exists as an independent company, which causes some critics to say, "See, we told you it wouldn't work." But that's not quite true. Although Control Data as such isn't around any more, there are at least 70 successful businesses that are spin-offs of the original company, Ceridian Corporation being the largest. Furthermore, Control Data continued to help many of these companies get started by investing in them.

There was bitterness when more than 2,000 people were laid off, while some high-level executives received lucrative "golden parachutes."

Worthy writes that Control Data's eventual financial troubles were seen by many "as conclusive evidence" that the notion of solving social problems through business means is "a dangerous delusion" and should serve "as a warning to other business leaders who might be tempted to follow Norris's lead."

Norris insisted that it is a legitimate business to meet the social needs of society, but you need to take a risk to do it. Berg used to say, "Some call us chintzy because we don't support the Guthrie Theater or the orchestra and the art institute as they think we should. They say it ought to be part of our social responsibility to support these organizations. We like to think that it is just as much an exercise of social responsibility to take larger than usual economic risks in order to provide jobs for people by investing in enterprises such as the Northside and Selby-Dale plants."

Norris did not operate by consensus. Perhaps there were times when it would have been better for him to curb his "compulsion to go north" when everybody else was going south. But then on the day before Norris's retirement was announced, the *Minneapolis Star and Tribune* would never have "mused on that rumor" and editorialized that "we're about to lose a congenitally opinionated, wonderfully outspoken and everlastingly imaginative corporate curmudgeon." And on the day of his retirement described him as "a man of many visions. Because Norris wasn't afraid of mistakes, he made them. Because he was a man of vision, he sometimes went too far. Because he was a self-confident leader, he wouldn't be second-guessed. As a result, some promises weren't delivered. But because of that courage, vision and leadership, Minnesota and America are richer in many ways because of him."

In February 1999, Allan B. Rossman of St. Paul wrote a letter for the Reader Response page of the *Star Tribune* business section in which he analyzed the decline of Control Data nearly fifteen years earlier: "It was the gradual increase and then excess of ineffective people becoming executives and their lack of leadership and direction of both products and employees."

"I worked at CDC for 18 years," he said. "I miss working with stimulating people in a flexible company driven by conviction and a mission set by Control Data founder William Norris. I've done quite well since then, but I've not found the same kind of flexible and stimulating work environment as existed at CDC.

"I recall riding in the elevator in the headquarters building very early one morning. Norris and I were the only ones in the elevator from the parking garage to the top floors. I felt like saying thank you for building this great company and that I was proud to be a part of it. But I didn't say it, and ever since I wished that I had."

Chapter 7

THE FERMENT OF THE 1970s

A s is often the case, the dictionary is a good place to begin. "Ferment:" "to undergo fermentation; to be in a state of agitation or intense activity." The decade of the 1970s—give or take a few years at either end—was such a time. A lot of things were happening. Some of them were interrelated. Others seemed to be totally independent and unrelated to each other. And yet, viewed in hindsight, they all seemed to contribute to the whole.

One problem in writing about the decade a quarter of a century later is that the people involved early on have differing recollections of the sequence of events.

Dominating the dialogues and conversations of the decade were such phrases as "corporate social responsibility," "public-private partnerships," "stockholders and stakeholders." These, too, were interrelated.

THE ROLE OF STUDENTS IN THE FERMENTATION

Except for campus uprisings, some corporate executives may never have been aware that students played a part in the fermentation of the 1970s. But as yeast has a way of working quietly, so there was an intellectual revolution going on among a relatively small group of business students at the University of Minnesota.

Providing the stimulation for this seemingly unnoticed activity was a young man by the name of Douglas Wallace, executive director of the University YMCA, adjacent to the University of Minnesota campus in Minneapolis.

Wallace held a divinity degree from Colgate Rochester Seminary in New York. A name closely associated with that seminary is Walter Rauschenbush, who in the early part of the century tried to mesh theological acumen with social responsibility. His influence was still felt on the campus when Wallace was a student there in the late 1960s.

Ordained as a Baptist minister, Wallace was attracted to opportunities where he could combine theological, ethical and social dimensions in parastructures dealing with the interaction of politics and business.

As the director of the YMCA Wallace attracted students with a wide range of interests. Some of them were business students who became interested in his Metro-Executive program, which placed students with local corporations for a year of internship.

Although there were other business internship programs throughout the country, the Minnesota program, as far as is known, was the only one specifically designed to deal with the question of ethics in business. "The program," Wallace explained, "was based on the assumption that future corporation executives would be illiterate in their management unless they had thought through the relationship between ethics and their business behavior."

The student interns were in an excellent position to act as catalysts. Since they were not beholden to the companies to which they were assigned, they could ask embarrassing questions at all levels of management.

At that time there were only two or three corporations that had departments dealing with these issues. Today virtually all of them have staff positions with responsibilities in this area.

"We didn't really plan it this way," Wallace recalls, "but a network developed among the few who did have those responsibilities. A department head of one company would talk with his counterpart in another company and say, 'I've got this student intern assigned to me and he is asking all kinds of questions,' and the reply he would get was, 'Oh, you've got one too; so have I.'"

Students weren't the only ones who were attracted by Wallace's message and program. Thomas Wyman, president of Green Giant, was the guest speaker one day at a YMCA luncheon where he spoke about Wallace's program. John Morrison, CEO of Northwestern National Bank, was in the audience. After lunch Morrison approached Wallace and said, "I'd like to talk to you in my office some time."

After three months of conversation Morrison offered Wallace a position as vice president for social policy at Northwestern National Bank. A social policy task force was formed and during the next six years all the employees of the bank participated in evaluating their activities in the light of ethical concerns.

When after a few years Morrison was promoted, Peter Gillette was named as his successor, and he followed through with the program started by Wallace. When Gillette was also promoted, a new president was brought in from a large bank in Chicago. According to Wallace and Gillette, the new president "didn't have a clue as to what all this talk of social policy was about." Within a short time he resigned, giving at least anecdotal evidence that there is something about the Minnesota business culture that is hard for outsiders to understand.

THE ITASCA SEMINARS

In 1970, Earl Ewald, CEO of Northern States Power, told Donald Imsland, one of his new staff members, "There's some kind of seminar for staff training scheduled at a YMCA camp in the Colorado Rockies. I'd like to have you go there and see if it's something NSP might do for our own staff."

When Imsland brought back a positive report and recommendation, Ewald decided this was not something NSP should do just for itself. Such an experience should be made available to other Minnesota corporations as well. He invited fifty CEOs to a week-long seminar at Itasca State Park in northern Minnesota, and thus the Itasca Seminar was born. It was held annually in the last week in September for more than 20 years.

Ewald was in favor of and committed to the idea, but he wasn't totally comfortable with NSP being its sole sponsor. His concern was one of both time and money. After all, asking fifty CEOs to give a whole week of their time for this kind of seminar was somewhat presumptuous. And for NSP to assume the entire cost might be questioned by some. But Ewald took the risk.

Several years later, David McElroy was named president of NSP. He shared Ewald's concerns. Neither of them had any doubts about the value of the program, but was this something for which NSP should spend it stockholders' money? Serious thought was given to discontinuing the seminar, or at least distributing the cost among other corporations. By this time the program had been so successful that other corporations asked if they could be included in sponsoring it.

The general management and program planning of the seminar was turned over to the Minneapolis Foundation, and in 1975, the following corporations and agencies shared in the planning and financial support: Bemis

Company, Federal Reserve Bank of Minneapolis, First Bank System, First National Bank of Minneapolis, First National Bank of St. Paul, General Mills, Honeywell, Inter-Regional Financial Group, Mayo Foundation, *Minneapolis Star Tribune*, Northern States Power Company, Piper Jaffray, the St. Paul Companies, and the Urban Coalition of Minneapolis.

About 80 people attended the seminar each year—approximately 40 representing business and industry, 10 from governmental institutions, 10 from educational institutions, 10 from religious institutions and 10 from community organizations. The supporting corporations underwrote "scholarships" for representatives from governmental, educational, religious and community organizations.

Each year a theme was selected that had practical significance for persons who were involved in the planning, policy and decision-making processes of major institutions. Among the themes that characterized the emphasis of the annual event were: The Life Systems, Growth and Survival, Corporate Social Concern, The Future of Institutions and Perspectives on America's Future.

The seminar featured nationally and internationally known speakers such as Elise Boulding, Mahub Ul Haq of the World Bank, Garret Harding of the University of California, Willis Harmon of Stanford Research, Thomas L. Hughes, president of Carnegie Endowment for International Peace, Chief Justice Annie R. Jiagge of Ghana and Carl H. Madden, chief economist of the U.S. Chamber of Commerce.

When Emmett Carson was named president of the Minneapolis Foundation in 1997, one of the first items on his agenda was to reexamine the Itasca Seminar. There was no question about its value. The question essentially was whether a program designed for the 1970s was equally valid for the 1990s, or whether the times changed sufficiently to call for a different approach and program to deal with different or even the same issues.

One major change certainly was the demands on CEO's time as well as the time of other corporate executives. Companies that had been mostly local 20 years ago were now regional, national or even international. No way would international-traveling CEOs or vice presidents from Minnesota corporations spend over half a day on a bus trip to Itasca, spend a whole week there and then another half day coming back home on the bus.

The discontinuance of the Itasca Seminar is not an erosion in commitment to what was being accomplished there. Nor was it entirely a time-commitment problem. "I like to quit when I'm ahead, when things are going well," Carson said, and there was evidence that the Itasca program had run its course. It was a matter of "been there, done that." Most of the Twin Cities corporate CEOs had been to Itasca and had sent their next level of leadership. It was time for a change and new structures.

What were some of those structures? Some are still in the process of formation. Among the leaders are such organizations as the Citizens League, Minnesota Center for Corporate Responsibility, Minnesota Meeting, Center for the American Experiment, and a variety of dialogues sponsored by colleges, seminaries and churches, to name but a few.

SPRING HILL, GEORGE LODGE AND HENRY SCHACHT

In 1976 George Cabot Lodge, a professor at Harvard Business School, was the keynote speaker at the Itasca Seminar. Judson Bemis admitted that he hadn't been in agreement with everything Lodge had said. "His big contribution to our own thinking," Bemis said, "was the importance he attached to having a representative from government be a part of our discussions." Lodge also spoke at the annual meeting of the Greater Minneapolis Chamber of Commerce. He made such an impression on Bruce Dayton, Tom Wyman and Judson Bemis, that they said, "We ought to invite him back some time and get a couple of others to hear him."

Lodge had said such things as, "The question of ownership of large publicly held corporations is causing [sharp doubts] about the role of stockholders and boards of directors, as well as about authority, legitimacy and responsibility of corporate management itself."

The stakes are high, Lodge had said. "Some institutions may be able to adapt to the new ideas that are emerging, survive and prosper. Others—notably corporations—may flee, searching the world for more hospitable ideological surroundings where the old structures are still acceptable." This was heady stuff for corporate executives.

Groups such as Doug Wallace's Metro-Interns asking difficult questions and Itasca Seminars' stimulating speakers such as George Cabot Lodge provided more than enough adrenaline for bringing key people together for more focused discussion and a plan for action.

And that brings us to a conference at Spring Hill Center, some 16 miles west of Minneapolis, on November 15 and 16, 1977, a notable event still remembered vividly by the "old-timers" of today (reference Appendix 2).

Henry Schacht, chairman and chief executive officer of Cummins Engine Company in Columbus, Indiana, was the keynote speaker. Cummins was known throughout the nation for having perhaps the most advanced understanding of corporate responsibility. But he felt quite at home in the Minnesota culture and even apologized for seemingly "carrying coals to Newcastle."

In many ways Spring Hill was a catalyst. There had already been a lot of thinking about corporate responsibility and about the necessity of giving as much attention to the "stakeholders" of corporations—customers, employees, and the community—as had generally been given to stockholders.

Considerable advance thinking had already been done on what was to become the Minnesota Business Partnership, but it was the Spring Hill Conference that brought the thinking to fruition.

MINNESOTA BUSINESS PARTNERSHIP

The article, "In Minnesota, Business Is Part of the Solution," written by Judson Bemis and John Cairns in the July-August, 1981 issue of the *Harvard Business Review* (HBR), described what happens "when CEOs of large companies join to work with—rather than ignore or oppose—government on socioeconomic issues."

The HBR article observed that in the post-Vietnam, post-Watergate era, the term "corporate social responsibility" was appearing frequently in the press. And corporate executives themselves became increasingly aware that business was being perceived as fundamentally and exclusively "part of the problem," if not *the* problem.

For years, the HBR article observed, business executives were convinced that they were being misunderstood, and that all would be well if they would only "stand up and tell their story." But their story seemed to fall on deaf ears. Perhaps their story wasn't so great after all. They decided to do something about it. That was the beginning of the Minnesota Business Partnership.

Business leaders themselves had begun to realize that too often business "tried to nip in the bud regulations or proposed legislation that seemed to oppose business interests—especially actions that might raise the cost of doing business." Perhaps that was why business's story was unconvincing to many.

A part of the Minnesota Business Partnership's mission was "to involve Minnesota corporate chief executives and their senior managers in public matters affecting not only their own business interests but also the interests of Minnesota and its citizens." They did not want to be known only as an anti-tax group, although taxes certainly would be a big issue. According to the *Harvard Business Review* article, "Even the recommendations on taxes covered aspects such as tax breaks and incentives for entrepreneurial growth, that were not directly connected with the concerns of large companies."

Top executives of member companies made frequent trips to the capitol in St. Paul. Carl Drake Jr., Chairman of The St. Paul Companies, explained the necessity of doing this. "It was the logical way to convince legislators that the business community was interested in true partnership to work on solutions to public problems."

A task force was appointed, chaired by Ray Herzog, then CEO of 3M Company. Seventy-five people from 20 companies were involved in various studies. The conclusions were presented at five simultaneous news conferences throughout the state.

The following listing of the twelve members of the original policy committee of MBP indicates the scope of participation from the business community:

Judson Bemis , chairman, executive committee, Bemis Company Inc.

Curtis L. Carlson, chairman and CEO, Carlson Companies, Inc.

Kenneth N. Dayton, chairman, executive committee, Dayton-Hudson Corporation

Carl B. Drake, president and CEO, The St. Paul Companies, Inc.

N. Bud Grossman, chairman and president, Gelco Corporation

Raymond H. Herzog, chairman and CEO, 3M Co.

E. Robert Kinney, chairman and CEO, General Mills, Inc.

Donald M. McCarthy, president and CEO, Northern States Power Co.

James P. McFarland, retired chairman and CEO, General Mills, Inc.

Louis W. Menk, chairman and CEO, Burlington Northern Inc.

Edson W. Spencer, president, Honeywell Inc.

William H. Spoor, chairman and CEO, Pillsbury Co.

With such a high level of participation by top business executives, they wouldn't dare to give the impression that they were concerned only with their own special interests.

Kenneth Dayton, at that time chairman of the executive committee of Dayton-Hudson, described how he viewed the mission of a business partnership:

"I dream of a day," he said, "when the two major forces in our society, government and business, will not be in frequent opposition to each other. It is my hope that [such a partnership] can play a constructive role in a dialogue and goal-setting process with government. It is my hope that it can do exactly the same thing with other elements of society that also have a big stake in the welfare of the state—with labor, with agriculture, with special interest groups, with educational interests and with the whole important and growing nonprofit sector of society."

The Minnesota Business Partnership was to be an action arm, composed of corporate CEOs, but it was to be more than a lobby group.

Agreeing with the principle but questioning the degree to which it can be carried out, Bernard Brommer, president of Minnesota AFL-CIO, opined that "as long as employees are viewed as an expense rather than an asset their jobs will always be in jeopardy and among the first cuts to be made to satisfy Wall Street's insistence on short-term profits."

FROM MINNESOTA PROJECT TO MINNESOTA CENTER

At the same time that the Minnesota Business Partnership was organized as an action group, a twin organization, The Minnesota Project on Corporate Responsibility, came into being as an educational arm. It was established to champion Minnesota values of good corporate citizenship.

An earlier suggestion for its name included the word "social," as in The Minnesota Project for Corporate Social Responsibility. "We fought hard for the removal of the word 'social,'" said Judson Bemis, "not because we didn't agree with it, but because it was too narrow. In those days 'social' was thought of largely in terms of philanthropy, the money that corporations gave to social causes. Our interests were far broader. We wanted to talk about such things as the relationship of stockholders and stakeholders and some of the ethical issues facing business."

In a more recent interview, Bemis said he was glad to hear that the meaning of "social" had expanded beyond philanthropy to include what had been argued for earlier.

"Maybe we can talk about corporate social responsibility now," said Bemis, but he also pointed out that it might be redundant, since responsibility, by definition, includes social responsibility.

The chief executive officers who met in those early discussions included Judson Bemis of the Bemis Company, Thomas Wyman of Green Giant, Bruce and Kenneth Dayton of the Dayton Hudson Corporation, C. Angus Wuertele of Valspar Corporation, Edson Spencer of Honeywell and John S. Pillsbury of Northwestern National Life. They did not begin with agreement on questions, much less answers. This was to be an educational experience. The common ground was a social vision and an emphasis on values. Their understanding of the relationship between society and business conceded a priority to society that business leaders all too often seemed to reject.

The reason it was called a project instead of a center at that time was that some felt it should be a temporary organization to deal with various projects. Its purpose should be to conduct a series of workshops that would help corporate CEOs understand the changes taking place in the business world, as well as the increasing interest and concern for ethics and values.

The idea was that all CEOs would be required to go through the workshop first, followed by other staff members from the company. According to Peter Gillette, one of the leaders in the movement, that procedure never really worked out. Frequently, after the CEOs went through the program, their relationship remained at a distance. Nevertheless some 2,000 corporate CEOs, vice presidents and other executive staff did go through a rigorous educational program.

Don Imsland of Imsland Associates was named executive director of the project. It never really had an office of its own. All business and administrative activities were conducted through Imsland's office.

After ten years, however, it became obvious that the changing world of business required continuing study and attention. More was needed than simply a series of projects addressed one after another. There needed to be a center at which long-range planning could be done. The ideal would be some form of affiliation with an existing organization, probably a university.

Possible affiliation was explored with three Twin Cities educational institutions: the University of Minnesota, the College of St. Catherine, and the University of St. Thomas. An affiliation with any of them could provide strength in several areas, all of equal importance. Financial needs were pressing. The Minnesota Project was supported by membership fees from local corporations and that membership was decreasing. An affiliation with a university could provide a source of additional income, as well as ready access to the academic community. And, perhaps most valuable of all would be the added recognition and sense of permanence that would come from being affiliated with a university.

The exploration came at a fortuitous time for the University of St. Thomas. It was building a new campus in downtown Minneapolis to house its rapidly growing graduate school of business, now the fourth largest in the country. It had recently launched the Koch Endowed Chair in Business Ethics. And, it was willing to make a significant financial investment to bring new stability to the cause. Thus, the Minnesota Project on Corporate Responsibility, formed in 1978, became the Minnesota Center for Corporate Responsibility in 1989.

After short interim presidencies by Paul Parker and Peter Gillette, Robert MacGregor was named president in 1991. During his eight-year presidency, the number of supporting member corporations more than doubled to

120. In 1999 he was named president emeritus of MCCR as he assumed the presidency of the Indevco Corporate Foundation in Lebanon.

In addition to its affiliation with the University of St. Thomas, MCCR has affiliated with the Carlson School of Management at the University of Minnesota to provide expanded services and research to the Minnesota business community.

Chapter 8

THE FIVE PERCENT CLUB AND THE MINNESOTA KEYSTONE PROGRAM^SM

During the interviews for this book, people were asked for their impressions about the philanthropic climate in Minnesota business culture. Their first reference—even people far away from Minnesota—almost invariably was to the "Five Percent Club." They had heard about it and it made an impression on them. They were to be reminded soon enough, however, that money isn't the whole story. But it is a big part of the story.

The name "Five Percent Club" says exactly what it is—Companies that give five percent of their before-tax domestic earnings to charitable, educational and cultural causes. Participants fall into three categories: Five Percent Participants; Two Percent Participants (those who contribute between two and five percent of their pre-tax profits); and Pledge Participants (those who have stated their intent to reach at least the two percent threshold in three years) (reference Appendix 3).

The essence of the idea was not new. As stated in chapter 4, George Draper Dayton and his wife set aside $500,000 in 1909, to which they added through the years; in 1918, the Dayton Foundation was incorporated. In 1946 Dayton's, then being run by the founder's five grandsons, made it official policy to give five percent of pre-tax profits through its foundation for charitable and benevolent causes. Other companies began to follow suit.

The idea was given a boost when President Lyndon B. Johnson addressed a gathering in Rochester, Minnesota. In vintage Johnsonian rhetoric, he challenged corporations to play a greater role in building healthy communities. A paraphrase of his comments would go something like this: "Look, you business people, you're always complaining that the government isn't doing enough. Our Congress passed a law to give you special tax breaks up to five percent of your profits if you will use it to build a better society. Why don't you get busy and do that?"

Bruce Dayton was at that meeting. While Dayton's and several other Minnesota corporations were already giving five percent of their pre-tax profits to philanthropy, the president's speech provided an impetus to encourage others to do likewise.

Another company to commit itself to this kind of five percent philanthropy was Graco, Inc., of which David Koch was the chief executive officer. His sense of personal stewardship expressed itself in the policy of the company.

In the mid-1970s Koch was elected president of the Greater Minneapolis Chamber of Commerce. Charles Krusell was the executive director of the Chamber. Krusell always asked the newly elected board chairman what he— in those days it was always a man—saw as the priority during his term of service. Koch expressed an interest in getting more companies to give five percent of their profits to the community.

So, according to Krusell, "We decided that during Koch's term of office, instead of having our normal kind of annual meeting, where we talk about how great the city is and show slides and all the rest, why don't we honor the five percent companies, the companies that have made the commitment to give five percent of their pre-tax profit to philanthropy. We didn't even know how many there were. We knew about Dayton's, of course, and Graco, Inc. and a few others."

Krusell wrote a letter to all the members of the Chamber and said, "If your company has made a commitment to give five percent of its profits to these causes, please let us know. We want to honor you at the annual meeting of the Chamber. At first some were reluctant to tell us, but twenty-three companies indicated that they had committed themselves to contributing five percent of their pre-tax profits to community projects.

The 1976 meeting of the Chamber attracted a sell-out crowd. "We were surprised ourselves at the huge audience," said Krusell. "The governor presented a plaque to the CEOs of the five percent companies, and the event got a lot of local and national publicity from the press. Inquiries came from all parts of the country. What was this Five Percent Club all about?" The time had come for a little more formal organization.

After its 1976 meeting, the Greater Minneapolis Chamber of Commerce assumed the responsibility for its administration and transformed the Five Percent Club into The Minnesota Keystone Program^{SM}, a name a bit more sophisticated perhaps, but still descriptive of the mission. Keystone was the operative word, defined as "the stone in the center of an archway that holds the other pieces in place, a symbol of bridging and strength—something on which the other parts of the wall depend for support."

The total membership in 1997 reached 253 in comparison with 23 when the club was organized in 1976. Of this total, 147 were Five Percent participants, 99 were Two Percent participants, and 7 were Pledge Participants.

The Keystone roster includes business in every industry category and size, from sole proprietorships to Fortune 500 companies. Of those on the roster, 21 percent employ fewer than l25 people, 26 percent employ 25-100, 27 percent employ 101 to 500, and 26 percent employ more than 500.

Since businesses are essential to the survival of Minnesota's communities, the Minnesota Keystone Program symbolizes the strong bridge of support between community needs and business resources. Healthy and safe communities help businesses thrive. Businesses and organizations are encouraged to make and maintain corporate investments in the community and are publicly recognized for those significant generous actions.

The concept has spread to other parts of the country. Ken Dayton and Dave Koch have been veritable "evangelists" to tell the story in other cities.

Although not all corporations in Minnesota are members of the Keystone Program or support the concept of the five percent club, enough of them do that they form a psychological, if not an official, peer group that persuades others.

Krusell tells the story of a chamber of commerce director of another large city who was impressed with the work of the five percent club and the Minnesota Keystone Program℠, and tried it in his city, but it failed.

"The difference between our success and his lack of success," said Krusell, "was that we had a sizeable number of companies of relatively equal size. For all intents and purposes, the other city, while large, was essentially a one-industry community. That company was so big that it virtually set the trend for thinking. And, since it was opposed to the five percent concept, none of the other companies would stick their necks out and assume a leadership position.

One of the reasons Emmet Carson, a relatively new Minneapolis resident, left his position at the Ford Foundation to become executive director of the Minneapolis Foundation, was the high regard in which Minnesota is held in philanthropic endeavors.

"Minnesota has a national reputation for being more generous, being more concerned about giving, being more volunteer and participation oriented and having an exceptionally strong arts community," Carson said. "I think that is generally born out by nearly every national study of giving and volunteer trends."

A new organization, "The One Percent Club," has been formed under the leadership of Joe Selvaggio. It represents a growing group of people of means who have a new vision for philanthropy as a transforming power in society. These people have committed themselves to give one percent or more of their net worth annually.

Within a year of its founding, more than 100 individuals and families committed themselves to this kind of giving. The idea was given further impetus at a luncheon at the Minneapolis Club on November 10, 1998, attended by more than 150 people. The highlight of the meeting was a panel of five business leaders who shared their general philosophy, its importance, and the excitement and personal joy of participating in this project.

In his comments, Kenneth Dayton, a former CEO of Dayton's, said, "I think the important thing is the principles our position enunciates, not the dollars or the percent. I don't think anyone of wealth has any right to gloat over what they give, because the poor do such a better job on a percentage basis than the wealthy do."

The other four members of the panel were Beck Horton, owner of Microton, a Minneapolis manufacturer of auto parts; Sylvia Kaplan, owner of The New French Cafe; Marilyn Carlson Nelson, chief executive of the Carlson Companies; and Winston Wallin, retired chief executive of Medtronic, Inc. Dayton outlined nine stages of philanthropy he and his wife Judy use as a guide for measuring their giving:

1. Minimal Response. This is the place most people start. It's not necessarily "the least you can get by with," but rather giving because you have been asked, and only because you have been asked—a good place to start but no place to stop.

2. Involvement and interest. As soon as one becomes involved as a volunteer in a non-profit organization, one's perspective changes dramatically and one's contributions generally increase equally dramatically.

3. As much as possible. Dayton says, "The transformation from Minimal Response to As Much as Possible is a truly remarkable one. It changes one's entire outlook on giving."

4. Maximum allowable. Giving the maximum the IRS allows for income tax deduction.

5. Beyond the Max. Dayton says, "One day in despair over IRA strictures, we decided to ignore the maximum allowable deduction and give what we wanted to give. It was a breakthrough experience. We began to see bigger and bigger chunks of so-called deductibility just disappear off our income tax returns."

6. Percent of Wealth. Says Dayton, "The trick is to determine the right percent-to-wealth standard for giving. Until we started to measure our giving against our wealth, we did not fully realize how much we could give away and still live very comfortably and well."

7. Capping Wealth. The Daytons are at Stage 7. They had to confront two questions: "How wealthy do we want to be?" and "How much money do we want to die with?" That means setting a limit on your wealth. "Capping your wealth" and giving away everything you earn beyond that figure.

8. Reducing the cap. "Whether we will ever have the courage and fortitude and intelligence to lower the cap as we get older, we cannot say," said Dayton. "But we can say that our thinking about the nine stages of giving and where we are on our course has at least put

the subject on the top of our table. We are comfortable discussing the subject."

9. Bequests. The ideal of course would be to give away our last dollar just before we die. Who wants to die rich or turn $1.10 over to Uncle Sam for every $1.00 we give to our heirs?

Despite the glowing reputation that Minnesota has gotten for being a leader in philanthropy, it would not be accurate to suggest that virtually everything originated here.

Recent developments that have caught the eyes and ears of Americans are the contributions (already totaling nearly $500 million) that Bill and Melinda Gates have made to various libraries and educational institutions. Of equal interest is the commitment of a number of the young millionaires at Microsoft to share their wealth as a debt they owe to society.

The fall 1997 issue of *The American Benefactor* lists the 100 most generous Americans whose giving ranges from $20 million to over one billion dollars.

The American Benefactor itself is a story of growing national interest in philanthropy. In the spring 1997 premier issue, Roberta d'Eustachio, founder and president, asks the question, "How do you change a donor who gives when asked, into a benefactor who takes the initiative, creates a legacy and makes a lasting difference?…To be a benefactor is to investigate, to discover, to muse upon a multitude of personal and financial issues—and once these issues are satisfactorily resolved, to take decisive action."

In the same issue, Nelson W. Aldrilch, Jr., editor in chief, describes the purpose of the magazine as "to celebrate, inspire and inform the act of giving. Note the choice of words. Not one suggests preaching, berating, or imploring…Our intent is to create a *community of the charitable*."

Minnesota expects to play a continuing and leading role in that community.

Chapter 9

MATCHING ETHICS AND ECONOMICS

This chapter is an interlude, essentially for the cynics. There will always be those who will insist that under capitalism it's simply impossible to be ethical. One clergyman put it this way: "Business has no moral vision. It is not interested in the common good. It wants only to maximize profit...The dominant business virtue is greed. I know of no corporation that has any sense of responsibility to our society, to future generations, or to the communities within which its factories or offices are located."

To challenge that viewpoint, one might begin with a definition and analysis of "maximize profit." If that would always mean maximize profit *no matter what*, then the cynics might have a point. However, if it means maximize profit in the long run, still making as much profit as possible but within the parameter of showing the utmost concern for employees, the customers and the public, then it's at least worth telling a couple of stories of a Minneapolis CEO, now retired, who conscientiously tried to factor his understanding of ethics into the economics of running a business.

One can still disagree with the decisions he made, but at least his experience should put to rest the attitude of those who feel business people in a capitalistic society simply cannot be guided by ethical concerns. In as much as these stories are not at all uncommon and could easily be told of numerous other CEOs, he has requested not to be identified.

THE MEXICAN MAQUILADORA

A *maquiladora* is a special business structure in Mexico that permits American companies to ship raw material into Mexico to be fabricated there and sent back to the United States with special tax advantages. Originally the maquiladoras were a string of factories on the Mexican side of the Mexican-American border. But today they have become far more numerous all over Mexico.

Just the mention of the concept raises all kinds of red flags that scream sweatshop labor and sacrificing American labor union jobs for low-paying jobs in Mexico, all to satisfy the greed of American capitalists. And there may well be situations in which those accusations are well-founded. But is it at all possible for a corporation to look on a relationship with a *maquiladora* as an opportunity in the best interest of both Mexico and the United States?

In the following story, a retired Minnesota CEO tells of his attempt to serve society through a *maquiladora* in Juarez, Mexico, and what he learned in the process:

> Our company chose a *maquiladora* to get our business into Central America. We chose it carefully. We interviewed extensively until we found one that seemed to be very advanced in caring for its employees, and so we started a very small operation that today employs over 1,000 people.

It was owned by a Mexican group of investors. However, we reserved the rights as far as we could under the law to attend to human resources policies.

We insisted that it meet the same health, safety and cleanliness standards as our own U.S. standards or state of Minnesota standards, but also our own internal company standards, which are even higher.

We insisted on a full battery of employee benefits to assist the people coming out of the rural provinces into Juarez, and we even tried to raise the wages. It turned out that we couldn't do that because this is controlled by the Mexican government. But we kept the pressure on the maquiladora employers to keep moving the standards up.

The Mexican government was saying, "Hey, don't do that, Yanqui. We're trying to build a world position where companies from all over the world are going to come here and manufacture. Maybe you don't like the rates that are being paid to the labor force, but you better understand that it's a hell of a lot better than the way they are living in the provinces; and that's why they flock to Juarez and all along the border to have jobs."

As the CEO of our company, I personally did most of the negotiations. There were some things we just couldn't do because of the Mexican government's regulations, but I just kept saying, "Let's monitor these operations. They've got to meet all of our safety and cleanliness standards."

Finally, when I was getting ready to retire, I made one more inspection trip, and I went down by myself. I was met by a very worried manager in the maquiladora, because they knew why I was there. I was the chief inspection agent on behalf of the company.

We spent two and a half days carefully going over all the safety and cleanliness regulations, the public health and all the programs that we provided, which were more extensive than those you typically find in the United States. We provided free lunches and free day care; we provided transportation to the factory. We provided a social worker and did all kinds of stuff. But the wages were the wages, and they were controlled by the government.

One of the things that was always brought up, and rightfully so, was the housing. It was terrible; so I insisted that I wanted to inspect the housing.

I had met the chap who took me out. He was a plain factory worker when we began ten years ago, and now he was a supervisor. We got into his car and we drove around. We looked at tin shacks and cardboard shacks, brick hovels and dilapidated stucco buildings, but we kept moving through even better housing.

"Well, you know," he said, "our work force comes out of the innards of the Chihuahua province and they typically are young. They come here when they are 17 or 18 years old, and they move in with relatives who are fellow village members from back home. So there may be three or four of them living in one room. And of course you think that's terrible."

I half-grunted, "Yeah."

"Then if it's a family and they begin to succeed," he said, "they'll rent one of these apartments, and maybe it's two rooms on the second floor, but it has running water and a toilet.

"Then the young men and women will marry and they continue to live with relatives for a period of time, but slowly and surely they begin to build their net worth and now they move into this little house.

"And finally," he finished by saying, "I'm going to take you to where I live."

We drove into a small housing development. All the property was separated by little walls, and here he lived in a wonderful house with three bedrooms, a couple of bathrooms, a living room, kitchen and dining room, a little patio and a little lawn. His wife was there. She works, but she came home for the day to meet me.

Their two daughters were there. Both go to good schools, both are bilingual, both of them will go to U.S. colleges.

And he said, "This is what we have achieved. And now I want to show you something."

He pulled out his wallet—it still brings tears to my eyes—and he said, "Here is a picture of my maternal family. My father died early."

And here was his mother in a dress that we would associate with Oklahoma in the thirties, a sack dress, a mother without shoes. They were standing in front of a mud adobe hut, and there were five children, all without shoes, all poorly dressed.

He said, "I am the oldest. Today I am a manager of your company. I have this house, and my girls are going to a U.S. college. My wife has a decent job and we have a full set of benefits that protects us.

"And here is my brother. With my earnings at your factory I brought him to Juarez. He is now an engineer. And here is my sister. She is next, and the two of us brought her to Juarez, and she is now a nurse, and the last two are now in college, and we're paying for them. And this is my mother."

He pulled out another picture. A nice little house.

"'You may not like our housing and our wage rates and all the rest may not meet your standards. Those are *your* standards. They're not ours, and what is happening here is good for us. Put that in your thinker when you go home and make your decision."

And to myself I said, "Yeah, you damn Yanqui. You need a little better understanding of imposing the values of your culture on values that other cultures might have."

Now was that American company making a profit? Of course it was. Was it making a maximum profit? It could probably have made more if it wouldn't have provided quite as many social benefits, but the CEO was matching economics with ethics.

And what about the American workers who might be losing jobs because their work could be done by cheaper Mexican labor? That's a crucial question to which we have to find a better answer in our increasingly competitive global market.

This is another illustration of where we need to take a long-range view. Grant for a moment that the Minnesota CEO was acting out of self-interest. But it was not self-interest only for himself. Some of that self-interest extended to American workers and to America as a whole, as well as to Mexico and Mexican workers. As someone observed, "Altruism is not to be sniffed at just because it helped you as well as others."

"If we think we have an immigration problem at our southern border now," the retired CEO said, "just remember that the Mexican population is increasing at unbelievable rates. In not too many years the population of Mexico is expected to double. What kind of immigration problems will we have at the border then? Or would we rather live in houses and communities surrounded by brick and stone walls, topped with barbed wires and shards of broken glass?"

Not only are we living in a global economy, but we are also living in a decreasing area of land available for housing, where we will have to live closer and closer together. Now that takes some real long-range thinking. Should we have more confidence in the long-range thinking of a Minnesota CEO or in the opinions of a liberal, activist clergyman who has lots of answers to complex economic problems, but who until he was well into middle age, still thought that *Standard and Poor* are adjectives?

GOOD INTENTIONS RUN UP AGAINST ECONOMIC REALITIES

A second personal experience story from the retired Minnesota CEO:

When I came to my former company, we were a transformer filter company with a labor-intensive product that required no manufacturing equipment. I arrived in midst of the 1970-71 recession, which was particularly hard on our products.

Our company, in fact, went technically bankrupt. It was saved only by one of the great civic leaders of the city, our major shareholder. He stepped up to guarantee our debt at the bank to keep our company alive. Somehow or other we survived thanks to his efforts, and I began looking at our work force in a small town where we manufactured all of our products. I was aware that their wages were quite low and that we had a bare-bones medical plan, no dental plan, no short-term or long-term life insurance, no disability plan, nor a retirement program. We just had none of the traditional benefits and I worried that we were not being socially just.

So I made a major effort and commitment to raise the wages and add a full benefit package for our employees, which meant of course that we had to succeed to afford this. We worked like dogs, all of us, and in fact we succeeded.

But two things were happening. We were able to continually increase wages of that work force, and we were able to add long-term and short-term insurance, disability and retirement programs, all the things that we now expect as benefits. I felt wonderful about having met my commitment and my goal, which I had published to the world to assure that a single wage in that town would afford a single parent and two children a standard of living above the poverty level. I thought that was my responsibility. That was great for me.

We had done a good job; we grew from $3 million to $21 million. We turned into a profitable corporation, and it was one of the highest quality operations in the country. We could sell our product to only a handful of customers because we were so expensive. You had to have a requirement for only the highest quality if you were to do business with that division. And we were delivering quality.

I could afford to do all of this because, fortunately, I had launched the rest of the company off on another endeavor, and that was succeeding brilliantly. It was the source of all our cash. It's true, our primary product was profitable, but only minimally so, and really in good conscience I couldn't justify the capital I was continually investing in the business just to keep it going.

So I was fulfilling my social conscience, but I was using the shareholders' money to do it, and I was doing something you should never do. I was endangering that operation because our customer base was getting smaller and smaller as fewer and fewer people could afford us.

But we were still growing the business because we were so good at what we did. We sold to the very biggest and the very best in the world. As a marketer, however, I knew all the time that we had to broaden our base, but we could never do it because our costs were too high.

Finally, we could no longer justify this. So bless my Board of Directors, I said to them, "You know we've built this up into a wonderful business. It's profitable. The employees are well cared for, but this is not where we should be investing a lot of our money. We need to find a new parent whose mainstream business is allied to what these people do and who want to have such a high quality work force they can use for something better."

So we asked the board to write off the whole operation in one fell swoop, write down all the assets to zero, so that next year we could go forward with absolute freedom to find a new parent for our employees, irrespective of return or price. All we had to do was to find the best match of a good wonderful corporation that would care for our employees and whatever we got for our corporation, Hallelujah, we could put it back in the books, and the board did that. That was a wonderful, wonderful thing.

And so we found a corporation that was the right mix, who picked up our people, and without missing a beat, we gave everyone severance pay according to seniority even though they were not going to lose a day of work, which was a boon for that small town. The new company stepped up and took wonderful care of these people, turned the operation into something else, went forth into the sunset singing and cheering, and we took the rest of our corporation and were better off and successful also.

When we sold the operation, we always obeyed all the governmental laws religiously, and one of them is that you never talk to a competitor. But when you're selling an operation, by very definition, you end up talking to competitors. They're the ones who want to buy your operation. We discovered that we were paying salaries to our work force about twice the going rate. No wonder we couldn't sell to anyone else.

Finally I reflected on what I had done. We had an operation in our small rural Minnesota town that largely was providing second jobs, second family incomes to wives of farmers and small town merchants, and this allowed them to have some medical benefits that they couldn't have as a small business person or a farmer. It provided a very nice second income, and it meant a lot to the employees themselves and to the community. But what I was doing was applying standards I had come to know at a Fortune 500 company in a city and trying to make something out of an operation that it was never intended to be. In my naiveté I was endangering all those jobs. It could just as well have gone out of business and everybody would have lost.

Here was a Minnesota CEO who understood that to be successful you can match ethics and economics. The question is, can that still be done in the increasingly competitive global economy in the coming generation? There are numerous CEOs in Minnesota, and undoubtedly elsewhere, who think it can.

Chapter 10

HOW DID WE GET TO BE THIS WAY?

Legacy is a good word. It helps to keep us humble. When you have a lot of goods things said about yourself, you are tempted to believe that they are all true, which they may well be. But you are also tempted to believe that they were all of your own doing. That also may be true, but not very likely.

As much as possible, all of the good things said about the Twin Cities so far in this book are true. The intriguing question is, "How did we get to be this way?" There is no simple answer, at least not one that passes the test of quantitative research or that draws straight lines between cause and effect.

The best we can do is to study the observations of scholars. One such scholar is James P. Shannon, who has held various positions as attorney, parish priest, Roman Catholic bishop, history professor, president of the University of St. Thomas, president and executive director of the General Mills Foundation and vice president of General Mills, Inc. He is also an authority on mid-19th century Minnesota history.

"If you want to understand what makes Minnesota what it is today and gives it such a reputation for corporate responsibility and public-private partnership," Shannon says, "you would do well to go back to the middle of the 1800s before Minnesota had even achieved statehood. That's a good beginning point for our legacy."

A key event was the 1851 Treaty of Traverse des Sioux between the U.S. Government and the Sioux Indians. The fairness of the treaty itself could be called into question. Years later Episcopal Bishop Henry B. Whipple excoriated it "as conceived and executed in fraud." The major effect of the treaty itself was that it opened the territory—and later, in 1858, when the territory became a state—to unbelievable opportunities for entrepreneurs who became the mainstay of the state's development.

The treaty gave some 20 million acres of land to the Minnesota territory in exchange for the Indians moving to the Black Hills. It was some of the richest farmland in the middle west—Governor Alexander Ramsey described it as the "extensive rich and salubrious region beyond the Mississippi." The chief attraction, however, was more than the abundance of productive land. The fact that the land was now actually owned by the government meant that farmers could buy it and get a deed which gave them protection of ownership.

Land was cheap, and two kinds of farmers were attracted: those who already owned farms in Ohio, Indiana, and Illinois, but who could get bigger ones in Minnesota; and second- and third-born sons from Scandinavia and Germany, where the custom was that the family farm went to the oldest son. In addition to bringing farmers, the land rush also brought merchants and sales people who would sell to farmers. All were pioneers with a high work ethic, one of the chief characteristics still ascribed to Minnesotans today.

"A salesman worth his salt could recognize that anyone who had anything to sell had an easy sale in Minnesota," says Shannon. "He didn't even have to be a salesman; all he had to do was just take orders."

The best example of that kind of entrepreneurship, according to Shannon, was Thomas Barlow Walker, who later gave his name to the Walker Art Museum. As a young man, he agreed to take a consignment of Ohio limestone from Xenia to Cleveland, Ohio, but he couldn't sell it. Someone told him that you can sell anything in Minnesota. So he took it by train to Galena, Illinois, put it on a boat and brought it up the Mississippi to St. Paul. There he sold it virtually over the weekend. Everybody seemed to need a grindstone.

These entrepreneurs, who were perhaps most responsible for putting their stamp on Minnesota, were largely from New England, and had already lived in the United States for several generations.

What made their adrenaline flow were the opportunities for commerce in the newly opened Minnesota Territory. They dreamed of building factories that would convert the products of the farms, mines and forests into marketable goods, as well as roads, railways and waterways to take them to all parts of the world. What characterized all of these early settlers was an incredible commitment to a work ethic.

These entrepreneurs had another contribution to make to Minnesota. Having settled and lived for several generations in the eastern cities of the United States, they knew the cultural requirements of a city: art, theater and music. When they arrived in Minnesota, they dreamed big. Visit the third floor of the Minneapolis Institute of Art today and you will see a model of the institute as it was originally planned. Before there were any pieces of art to exhibit, plans were already on the drawing board for a museum three times the size of the present building.

Another characteristic that these New Englanders brought with them to Minnesota is described by Bruce Dayton as their Calvinist conscience.

One tenet of Calvinism is that a person's wealth is an evidence of the approval and blessing of God, a blessing that carries with it the responsibility to use this wealth for the common good of all. One Presbyterian cleric simplified the concept to "Work as hard as you can, make as much money as you can, use as much of the money as you can to serve others." That sounds like a forerunner of current Minnesota philanthropy.

Geography itself played a role in determining the characteristics of Minnesota. Despite its relatively small population, it developed into a major hub for the whole upper Midwest—Wisconsin, Iowa, North and South Dakota and Montana. Even when the population approached four million, the state was large enough that it didn't have to be crowded. It's not the endpoint of most journeys. People pass through the state. The hardy ones— and the climate demands that they be hardy—who do stay, and stay for generations, are for the most part quite homogenous. While this makes for stability, at least until recently it could give the illusion that the state had no racial problems or biases. Problems that face the more heterogeneous and crowded communities of the East and West coasts are now coming to Minnesota and other midwest states.

Don Imsland, executive director of the Minnesota Project on Corporate Responsibility during its first twelve years (1978 to 1990), traces the history of Minnesota's development of corporate social responsibility through four generations and identifies them broadly as entrepreneurs, philanthropists, social activists and expansionists.

"It's essentially a story about principles," says Imsland. "It begins with the early settlers of Minnesota. This first generation of entrepreneurs had the ability to convert natural resources into economic value, which resulted in an unusually large number of successful corporations. Their business success was accompanied by a set of deeply held religious values that are the basis for the large number of private and corporate foundations located in the state."

There were the families (Blandin, Cargill, Dayton, Hamm, Hill, McKnight, Pillsbury, Wilder) with their deep-seated values. Another successful entrepreneur was the late Atherton Bean, for many years the CEO of International Multifoods, and remembered for his deep interest in corporate citizenship.

Then came the corporate entities that embodied these values and grew into national and international giants, extending these values to other corporate entities throughout the world.

Imsland describes the second generation as the philanthropists, the stewards of the economic success of the first generation. They created wealth, but for a purpose—to promote the common good. George Draper Dayton was a prime example. But the generosity didn't end with the second generation. Not only are the seeds sown then still bearing fruit, but new seeds continued to be sown through the coming generations.

In 1998 the Minnesota Council on Foundations listed 158 foundations in the state. Of that number, 78 were listed as private and family foundations, 52 were corporate foundations, and 22 were community and public foundations. The annual grants from private and family foundations range all the way from less than $100,000 to more than $75 million. For instance, the McKnight Foundation, the largest of the family foundations, made grants of $76.2 million during 1997. That's more than a million and a half a week.

Each foundation sets up its own grant policy to determine what kinds of projects it should fund. The companies that set up those foundations were built on a value system of corporate responsibility and a high level of business ethics that enabled them to do well.

The third generation included the social activists of the 1960s and 1970s. They brought corporate response to the social crisis of the times and fostered public-private initiatives to deal with them.

The fourth generation is dominated by the expansionists, bringing the infusion of local values to a global scene. (See Chapter 11, "The Minnesota Legacy Goes Global" and Chapter 13, "Where Do We Go from Here?")

It should not be surprising that religion played a leading role in shaping the values of Minnesota. When James Shannon became executive director of the Minneapolis Foundation, he identified ten people who had established a reputation of being successful in business and also of using their wealth for philanthropic causes. Although most of them considered themselves religious, only two—George Draper Dayton and Thomas Barlow Walker—explicitly connected their philanthropy and social theory with their religion.

By contrast, James J. Hill, owner of the Great Northern Railroad, although not a Catholic, became a heavy contributor to Catholic causes. He fell in love with Mary Theresa Meheagan, whose mother owned a rooming house in St. Paul. Both mother and daughter were devout Catholics.

Hill soon discovered that if he wanted to marry the daughter he would have to make his peace with the Catholic Church. He approached her priest, Father Caillet, and said he would like to have him make arrangements for Mary Theresa to go to finishing school in Milwaukee, run by Catholic nuns.

Hill is generally identified as one of the "robber barons," but his generosity to the Catholic church shows another side of him. Beginning in 1880 he built all five buildings at St. Paul Seminary, giving as his rationale, "My wife is a member of the Catholic church and my children and I have lived in a very devout Catholic family. This seminary is a gift to the church that trained and educated my wife. I want to recognize what the church has done for her and what she has done for me."

At that time, America was filling up with an abundance of people trained in Europe. Many of them were Catholics. Hill reasoned that if they were to become useful and vote-casting citizens in a democratic society, they had to have some kind of instruction in the system. The one person in town they respected was the priest.

"I want to make it possible to train the priests who train the people," Hill said. His critics said, "Train these people to become docile workers."

Although Hill never joined the church, for a time he had a friendly relationship with Archbishop John Ireland and supported Catholic endeavors. But the two had a falling out over the building of the St. Paul Cathedral. Hill thought that the cathedral Ireland was planning was far too big. He promised to give $250,000 if the Archbishop would build a smaller one.

Their relationship continued to sour, to the point that Hill and his office staff talked about the Archbishop in code language. They didn't want to openly refer to him as Archbishop Ireland, and to speak of him as AI might be a little too obvious. So the code for the archbishop in interoffice communication between Hill and his staff became "Asperity Ipswich," words that Shannon describes as "faintly pejorative." Solemnity can have humorous moments.

An insight into Hill's philanthropic philosophy is evidenced by the way he passed on his estate to his family after his death. It divided his assets among his wife and children, stipulating that upon their death the residue of their estates should go to worthy causes. Minnesota continues to be the beneficiary of Hill's philanthropic generosity that was matched by his hardball business deals.

"A sense of social responsibility is a religious phenomenon," says Dr. David W. Preus, pastor of University Lutheran Church of Hope in southeast Minneapolis during the 1960s. In 1973 he became the Presiding Bishop of The American Lutheran Church. While pastor of University Church of Hope he was also president of the Minneapolis School Board and served on the city's Board of Estimate.

Preus paid tribute to the Catholic, Protestant and Jewish communities for their solidarity and contribution to the social fabric of the state. "We were fortunate to have those New Englanders with their strong Calvinistic theology," said Preus. "Their sense of duty was great. Northern European Lutheran immigrants reflected a strong cooperative movement. The Catholics built solid communities. The religious rootage of all groups embodied just plain hard work and the assumption that this was what God wanted them to do."

Rabbi Max Shapiro, for many years the senior rabbi at Temple Israel, served as a vital link between the Jewish and Christian communities. The Jay Phillips family was well known for its participation in religious activities in the Jewish community, but also for its support of social programs throughout the city. Mr. Phillips founded the Phillips Family Foundation in 1944 which was instrumental in the building of Mount Sinai Hospital in Minneapolis. The foundation continues to support worthy projects with its assets of more than $150 million.

Some of the relationships between churches, community and business developments occurred by serendipity. For instance, one Sunday back in the early 1950s, Stuart Leck heard a particularly inspiring sermon by the Rev. Richard Raines at Hennepin Avenue Methodist Church in Minneapolis. This experience, which he shared with others, led to the formation of the Citizens League in 1952. Leck served as its first president.

The League has always been a place for people who are serious about public issues. In fact, many community leaders in government, politics and business got their start in public affairs through the Citizens League. Over the past four decades the League has produced over 400 citizen-based research reports which have helped shape Minnesota's public policy.

Churches and ministers often become safe places and people where and with whom new ideas can be tested out. Again, it was at Hennepin Methodist Church that Leslie Park first shared his designs for the Minneapolis skyway system, which together with the St. Paul skyways are now the largest in the world.

While the churches themselves were not the instigators of the Citizens League, the skyway system, or a variety of other civic or business programs, through their regular ministries members were reminded of their duties to the community.

In reflecting on his own relationship with the corporate executives who were members of his congregation, the Reverend Donald Meisel, for many years the senior minister of Westminster Presbyterian Church in Minneapolis, said he did not see himself as their confidant in matters of the corporate world.

"I tried to make all of my sermons relevant to today's world," he said, "and occasionally some of my members did tell me that my sermons were meaningful to them for the difficult business decisions they had to make." Meisel considered a major contribution of the congregation to the community to be the Thursday noon Westminster Town Hall Forum which usually packs the church for speakers of national and international stature. The program is broadcast live on public radio, made possible with sponsorship from Minnesota corporations.

Father Robert Cassady, senior pastor of Our Lady of Grace Catholic Church in Edina, reports that corporate executives who are members of the parish will use him on occasion as a sounding board as they struggle with ethical problems relating to their business.

Archbishop Emeritus John R. Roach, former president of the National Council of Catholic Bishops, reports a good relationship with corporate leaders during the 1980s while the bishops were developing their statement on "Economic Justice for All." They obviously couldn't get all of their theological and economic viewpoints to match, but they learned from each other.

"The corporate executives had particular difficulty in understanding, or at least accepting as a major part of the church's role its ministry and commitment to 'the poorest of the poor,'" Archbishop Roach said.

Many churches, large and small, of all denominations, sponsor adult education programs and forums that include discussions of current affairs and the relation of religion and theology to the corporate world.

The membership in Twin Cities churches includes leaders in various business and government organization. For instance, House of Hope Presbyterian Church in St. Paul has attracted such members as former vice presidents Hubert Humphrey and Walter Mondale and U.S. Chief Justice Warren Burger.

In addition to sponsoring specific seminars, the church, by its very presence, provides an opportunity for reflection. Father John Forliti, pastor of St. Olaf Catholic Church in downtown Minneapolis, said now that St. Olaf has become accessible via the skyway system, an increasing number of people are drawn to spend quiet, meditation time in the church.

The Rev. Lamar Hamilton directs an organization known as Church Metro, with a budget of $500,000. Its mission is to bring business people together for a better understanding of the spiritual and religious dimension of their daily work. Some of the city's leading CEOs, such as Addison (Tad) Piper of Piper-Jaffray, Kenneth Melrose of The Toro Company and William George of Medtronic—to name but a few—have brought their personal testimony of the importance of spiritual values in their management style.

The story of the late Harry (Bobby) Piper is particularly noteworthy. Already past middle age, he enrolled for a three-year course at United Theological Seminary in New Brighton, not because he wanted to become a clergyman, but because he wanted a theological grounding to help him think through his responsibility in regard to his wealth.

It is noteworthy that a number of leaders of non-profit agencies dealing with social issues are clergypersons or at least have had a theological education. Some of them were ordained and served in the church at least for a time, such as James P. Shannon, a Roman Catholic bishop. Robert

MacGregor, president of the Minnesota Center for Corporate Responsibility, was formerly pastor of Andrew-Riverside Presbyterian Church in southeast Minneapolis. Others include Russell Ewald, former Episcopal rector and later executive director of the McKnight Foundation, and Douglas Wallace, ordained as a Baptist minister, who has conducted seminars on ethics.

Some who were theologically trained included Donald Imsland, the first executive director of the Minnesota Project on Corporate Responsibility, the forerunner of MCCR; Thomas Beech; and Jerry Catt, who served for a time as director and assistant director of the Minneapolis Foundation.

Reell Precision Manufacturing Company (RPM) in St. Paul is an unusual example of a corporation committed to religious principles, even to the extent of having a reference to God in its mission statement. Incorporated in 1970 by three men, Dale Merrick, Bob Wahlstedt and Lee Johnson, each investing $1,000, its chief product is high quality clutches used by manufacturers in all parts of the world.

The company is committed to Judeo-Christian values, and top management is required to have an understanding of and commitment to those principles and values. However, it has stopped short of calling itself a "Christian" company.

"In the first place," Wahlstedt says, "only individuals can be Christians. But more importantly, the company is committed to respect the value of all individuals, regardless of faith or lack of faith."

Even the company's name reflects its sense of values. While Precision Manufacturing describes the company's activity, it was looking for an acronym. Merrick suggested that RPM would be easy to remember, but deciding on an "R" word was difficult. After going through the entire "R" section of the dictionary without finding the "right" word, Johnson found a German dictionary and discovered the word "Reell" (pronounced Ray-el) which means honest, dependable or having integrity. Hence the name, RPM, Reell Precision Manufacturing.

The company's values relate to its treatment of employees as well as to the quality of its products. One of its underlying policies is that as long as the company is making a profit, it will not lay off any workers. When hard times hit—and they have at various times during its short 27-year history—all employees, starting with the president, will take a cut in salary rather than lay off any worker. Every effort will be made to keep this salary policy in the future, which may be more difficult in an increasingly competitive global economy. The number of employees has gone from three to 75.

There is little if any doubt that religion has played a significant role in inculcating the value system of the Minnesota business community.

Colleges and universities in the Twin Cities and out-state areas also played a leading role in developing a climate that fostered a high level of ethics and corporate responsibilities. Two universities, the University of Minnesota and the University of St. Thomas, have chairs endowed by business or family foundations.

David Koch, chairman of Graco Inc., and his wife, Barbara, have created the Koch Endowed Chair of Business Ethics at the University of St. Thomas, currently held by Dr. Kenneth Goodpaster. The University of St. Thomas, the fourth largest graduate school of business in the country, also offers an MBA course entitled *Spirituality at Work* that is becoming increasingly popular among students.

The H. B. Fuller Foundation has endowed the Elmer L. Andersen Chair of Corporate Responsibility at the Carlson School of Management at the University of Minnesota. Andersen was formerly chairman and CEO of H. B. Fuller Company and also served a term as governor of Minnesota. At present, Dr. Norman Bowie holds that chair.

Business education at both universities has been enhanced greatly through gifts from business and community leaders. For example, the University of St. Thomas was awarded a $30-million gift from a family committed to supporting management education based on values and ethics.

The University also received a $50-million gift, in part to support entre-preneurial education, from Best Buy founder, chairman, and CEO Richard M. Schulze and his wife Sandra. The Carlson School of Management at the University of Minnesota owes a tremendous debt to Curtis L. Carlson and the Carlson Companies which have given over $50 million and led a fund drive that netted more than $300 million. Support for both institutions reflects the commitment of business leaders to give back to the community and to encourage the next generation of business leaders by their example.

In addition, liberal arts colleges and universities throughout the state provide courses with an emphasis on business ethics. They include Augs-burg College in Minneapolis; Bethel College, the College of St. Catherine, Macalester College, Concordia University and Hamline University in St. Paul; Carlton College and St. Olaf College in Northfield; Gustavus Adol-phus College in St. Peter; St. John's University at Collegeville; Bethany Lutheran College. Mankato; Concordia College, Moorhead; and St. Mary's College, Winona.

In addition, Minnesota is blessed with numerous colleges and univer-sities that recognize the importance of liberal arts as a basic necessity for the social fabric of the state. While it may be difficult at times to draw a direct cause and effect line between their normal class instruction and its produc-tion of graduates committed to ethical principles of business there can be little doubt that these educational institutions have played a leading role in developing a Minnesota culture for responsible corporate citizenship.

Chapter 11

THE MINNESOTA LEGACY
GOES GLOBAL

O ne Minnesota CEO said it this way. "Just who do these guys from
Minnesota think they are that they can superimpose their values
on countries with totally different cultures?"

Well, let's hear from some people outside of Minnesota.

In a letter of May 25, 1993, to Minnesota Governor Arne B. Carlson,
Ryuzaburo Kaku, then chairman of the Canon Company in Japan, described
a meeting at which the speakers were Charles M. Denny Jr., chairman of
ADC Telecommunications, Inc. in Minneapolis, and Robert W. MacGregor, president of the Minnesota Center for Corporate Responsibility.

"Both gave lasting impressions," Kaku wrote. "Denny spoke to a symposium, which had an audience of three hundred, including four ambassadors and diplomatic corps from ten countries. It was broadcast via NHK,
Japan's public broadcasting corporation to Japan, Asia and Oceani.

"The two gentlemen also introduced the *Minnesota Principles* in China
at the Guangdong Economic Seminar, an event sponsored by Governor

Zhu Shinlin of the Guangdong province and held before an audience of high officials of the provincial government and mayors of major cities.

"Postures and contributions to the communities by the members of the Minnesota Center for Corporate Responsibility are exemplary models for businessmen of the world. I am much encouraged that these principles are now being introduced widely to the world."

There is a refreshing sign of hope in Japan. It's called *kyosei* (kee-oh'-say)—an ideal that parallels concepts promulgated by the Minnesota Center for Corporate Responsibility. It's essentially the story of Canon, noted for cameras and office equipment, and its chairman from 1977 to 1997, Ryuzaburo Kaku. *Kyosei* is the Japanese word for living and working together for the common good. It's also a story of the compatibility of doing well and doing good.

Kaku tells the story under the title, "The Path of Kyosei" in the July-August 1997 issue of *Harvard Business Review.*

"Too few politicians in Japan today are capable of solving global problems," says Kaku. "The mantle of leadership has fallen onto the shoulders of corporations."

Canon was already a success before *kyosei* was introduced. Founded in Japan in 1937 as a manufacturer of high quality cameras, Canon quickly diversified and became a leading international company.

In 1975 the company ran out of cash, and for the first time had to suspend dividends. On the basis of some suggestions that Kaku made to turn the company around, he was made president. According to his article in *Harvard Business Review,* he introduced two important changes: first, to redouble efforts in research and development, and second, to place greater emphasis on Canon's social responsibilities and make tackling the world's many problems a vital part of Canon's mission. He introduced the concept of *kyosei,* which blended Canon's technological leadership with the belief that "we could work with others to improve the world."

The reason the Kaku and Canon story of *kyosei* is at all related to the Minnesota unique business culture is that the two are so similar in their understanding of corporate social responsibility, and that Kaku himself has described the Minnesota Center for Corporate Responsibility as providing an "exemplary model for businessmen of the world."

The five stages of corporate *kyosei* embody some of the same concepts promoted by MCCR.

1. The first of these is a sound business foundation that provides economic survival. Companies need a predictable stream of profits to establish strong market positions. In so doing, however, Kaku says they tend to exploit their staffs and create labor problems.

    "For instance," Kaku said, "I feel that some U.S. companies take the profit motive too far when they lay off workers to increase profits and at the same time pay large bonuses to their CEOs. Making a profit is only the beginning of a company's obligations. As they mature, businesses need to understand that they play a role in a larger global context."

2. Cooperating with labor. Canon was the first major company in Japan to go from a six-day work week to a five-day work week. "We were all against it at the time, and said that Canon would not be able to make a profit that way," says Kaku, "but we found after we made the change that Canon's productivity actually rose. By caring for our employees, we have found that they take care of the company, and we all benefit as a result."

3. Cooperating outside the company. Competitors are invited into partnership agreements and joint ventures, which result in higher profits for both parties. Community groups become partners in solving local problems.

4. Global activism. By cooperating with foreign companies, large corporations not only can increase their base of business but also can address global imbalances.

5. The government as a *kyosei* partner. When a company has established a worldwide network of *kyosei* partners, it is ready to move to the fifth stage, using their power and wealth to urge national governments toward rectifying global imbalances. Kaku admits that fifth-stage companies are very rare.

"I recently met with a group of 35 CEOs from Europe, Japan and the United States," Kaku said. "We talked about the role of global corporations in world affairs. I asked them if they thought *kyosei* had any chance of becoming popular in the United States. I expressed my doubts and cited recent downsizing practices there. I was pleasantly surprised to hear that my audience was against that approach to do business. In fact, they supported the concept of *kyosei*. That was heartening."

The jury is still out in Japan, as well as in the United States, both in the definition of corporate social responsibility, as well as in a willingness to commit energy to further the idea.

Keidanren, the Japan Federation of Economic Organizations, is also committed to many of the same principles as the Minnesota Center for Corporate Responsibility and the Caux Round Table. Their *Charter for Good Corporate Behavior* adheres to ten principles, including a commitment to the concept of the Minnesota Keystone Program℠, beginning at the one percent level.

THE MINNESOTA PRINCIPLES

In 1992 a group of Minnesota business leaders, interested in fostering the fairness and integrity of business relationships in the emerging global marketplace, developed a statement that came to be known as *The Minnesota Principles.*

It was described as a "statement of aspirations, not meant to mirror reality, but to express a standard against which our often inadequate performance can be held accountable."

Since that statement grew out of the experience and values of Minnesota business people, it was, therefore, local. However, the developers of the statement said, "We think it also fairly represents ethical values arising from the culture of North America."

The statement had a twofold purpose: (1) To describe the ethical systems of each trading area such as to be aware of and sensitive to the behaviors most valued by trading partners from other parts of the world; and (2) To begin a process, based on this statement, that identifies shared values and reconciles differing values so as "to move toward developing a world standard of business behavior that is acceptable to and honored by all."

Underlying the purpose of the statement was the rationale that virtually all business has global implications, and raises such questions as, "Is it ethical to eliminate jobs in one country just because they can be done at lower cost in another country?" The question is not simply rhetorical, assuming that the answer is obviously "no."

Nor does the statement assume that there is a ready answer. Its purpose is to be one tool in addition to others in a search for an answer.

The Minnesota Principles advocated five propositions:

1. Stimulating economic growth is the particular contribution of business to the larger society. Profits are fundamental to the fulfillment of that function.

2. Business activities must be characterized by fairness, which includes equitable treatment and equality of opportunity for all participants in the marketplace.

3. Business activities must be characterized by honesty, which includes candor, truthfulness and promise-keeping.

4. Business activities must be characterized by respect for human dignity. They should show a special concern for the less powerful and the disadvantaged.

5. Business activities must be characterized by respect for the environment. They should promote sustainable development and prevent environmental degradation and waste of resources.

Participants—seventeen altogether—in developing the statement were drawn from a wide variety of Minnesota companies. They did not speak for their companies; nor did their participation indicate complete agreement with the final document. The Minnesota Center for Corporate Responsibility takes full and sole responsibility for the publication of the statements.

Charles M. Denny, Jr., a leading participant in the drafting of the statement, gives this overview for the statement:

We came to the conclusion that business leaders have three primary tasks, three public responsibilities:

1. We should not be ashamed of business' ability to create wealth. Sometimes business people are led to feel guilty just by the very fact of creating wealth. Business creates wealth which creates prosperity, and prosperity is good for the nation.

2. But there must be a second and co-equal responsibility, and that is the just distribution of that prosperity. Most business people might say, 'Well I have nothing to do with that. That's a government issue.' But we as leaders do in fact through the years make decisions that may be small in specific ways, but in the aggregate are very important. One of those is how we distribute wages and compensation within our firms. And another is obvi-

ously how we act in the polemical spectrum in urging our government to behave in one way or the other in the distribution of our nation's wealth. That speaks to justice.

3. Third and equally important are the efforts within the corporation with its money, through its employees and through its individual leaders to create community. This relates to the non-material aspects of life that knit us together as a society and that assists in the creation of healthy families, healthy individuals, and through them healthy societies.

That tripartite division of our labor is a very important concept; and it really says to the individual business leader, 'Hey, it isn't good enough that your firm is doing brilliantly and that you're making a ton of money. You have these other two aspects that you need to be concerned about.'

Because if you and your progeny do not want to live behind guarded walls on top of which are broken glass and barbed wires, if you want to be able to drive without fear into your city to enjoy public entertainments, then you're going to have to do these other things. You can't hide.

The widespread use of the *Minnesota Principles* came as a surprise even to those who developed the statement.

THE CAUX ROUND TABLE

On a larger scale, the Caux (coe) Round Table (CRT), with headquarters in Caux, Switzerland, is in a sense the global counter-part of the Minnesota Center for Corporate Responsibility. The CRT also adopted a "Principles for Business" (reference Appendix 4) statement, and in the introduction to its document, it expresses a "substantial debt" to MCCR for the "language and form" of its statement. MCCR, with assistance from Dr. Kenneth

Goodpaster, Koch Chair in Business Ethics at the University of St. Thomas Graduate School of Business, played the lead role in facilitating the CRT discussions that integrated stakeholder concepts from the *Minnesota Principles* with ideas from Europe and the concept of *kyosei* from Japan. In effect the CRT statement is an adaptation of the MCCR statement in a broader arena, as evidence that there are some broad values that are common to all cultures.

The Caux Round Table was launched in 1986 by senior business leaders from Europe, Japan and North America to address global issues affected by the performance and conduct of international business. Initially concerned to promote solutions to the tensions arising from trade imbalances, the CRT has monitored the continuing changes in the economic and political landscape. Its influence has grown through the formulation and wide circulation of its statement on *Principles for Business.*

The CRT believes that global business stands at the crossroads of the fundamental changes taking place in the world. It believes that business has a crucial role in helping to identify and promote solutions to issues that impede the development of a society that is more prosperous, sustainable and equitable.

Globalization is moving forward relentlessly, with freer movement of people, capital, jobs, trade and information. Global businesses operate in essentially a borderless manner and have considerable power to effect change while the direct role of nation states internationally is diminishing. As reluctant as some corporations have traditionally been to go beyond their operational objectives, the time has come for the roles of corporations, governments and other institutions to be significantly redefined—a time for new partnerships and greater cooperation on a global level.

Business is often the first contact between nations and, by the way in which it causes social and economic changes, has a significant impact on the level of fear or confidence felt by people worldwide. Members of the

Caux Round Table place their first emphasis on putting one's own house in order, and on seeking to establish what is right rather than who is right.

CRT proposes seven general principles as guidelines for appropriate corporate conduct (See Appendix 4 for complete text of the Caux Round Table *Principles of Business* and Appendix 5 for a document entitled *The Critical Role of the Corporation in a Global Society*).

These Caux Round Table *Principles for Business,* based on the *Minnesota Principles,* have been translated into at least 12 languages, and additional translations are being made. More than 100,000 copies have been distributed in print and via the Internet. They are found in leading textbooks used in business schools around the country. They are being used by the Catholic school system in Latin America. A Chinese translation, printed in Hong Kong, is distributed throughout Asia; and an Arabic translation, printed in Beirut, is distributed throughout the Middle East. Other initiatives, such as regional CRT offices in Mexico, Thailand, and Singapore are under way to further distribute these principles.

Consider also that of the approximately 30 business leaders from the United States who have participated in CRT activities during the last ten years, half of them have been from Minnesota.

Furthermore, Winston Wallin, former CEO of Medtronic, is the chairman of the Caux Round Table, facilitating the same kind of dialogues that have been going on in Minnesota for the past 20 years. At present, the Caux Round Table has a regional secretariat office in the United States, Europe and Japan. Michael A. Olson of Minneapolis, Minnesota, is the executive director of the Americas.

The Critical Role of the Corporation in a Global Society, a position paper of the Caux Round Table, suggests that we are at a "major turning point in history, a time that occurs only once every hundred years or so, when adequate vision is lacking, leadership is weak, new technology sweeps across nations, gaps widen between people, laws and institutions break down, values weaken, crime and corruption and human relations falter."

There is a time when commitment comes before understanding. If action to remedy the situations just described were to wait until we had complete understanding or all the answers, it would never happen. Neither the CRT nor MCCR pretends to have all the answers to the world problems. But they have a commitment. Understanding and answers are bound to come.

Totally apart from the formal endorsement of the *Minnesota Principles* by the Caux Round Table, the message of Minnesota in yeast-like fashion has already found its way into the business philosophy of certain transnational corporations.

Prior to the 1989 hostile take-over of the Pillsbury Company in Minnesota by Grand Metropolitan from England, Grand Met had done considerable homework. They did not want to have the same experience that the Dart Company of the Haft family had several years previously in their failed attempt of a hostile take-over of Dayton-Hudson.

Grand Met became aware of the difference between the cultures in Europe and the United States (particularly Minnesota) in the way they dealt with social issues. In Europe, the governments take a more active role in solving social problems than is the case in the United States where the business community often takes the lead or at least works in close partnership with the government.

While the negotiations were going on during the hostile take-over of Pillsbury, Grand Met assigned Raymond Krause, director of government relations for Pillsbury, to help the British company adapt its practices to the Minnesota way of relating to the community. Since that time Grand Met has adapted many of these practices to its operations in other countries. Minnesota corporations practice the same principles for business in their worldwide activities for which they have become known in the United States. The Minnesota legacy is indeed going global.

Chapter 12

A TIME FOR REAPPRAISAL

What some would call Minnesota's vaunted reputation for corporate and public leadership and partnership may be coming in for reappraisal. Under front-page headlines, "Today's Civic Enterprise Murkier, But Less Top-down," in the February 19, 1998, issue of *Minnesota Journal*, a publication of the Citizens League, Charles Neerland, a principal with Neerland & Ovaas, Inc., asks the question, "Are we doing better now than we did in the past?"

His answer is yes and no. "In the old days—the late 1960s, 1970s, and 1980s," says Neerland, "we did things differently than we do them now in matters of civic enterprise and our blessed public/private partnerships. But better? In some ways perhaps; in other ways maybe not."

The headline captured the ambiguity. The way we do things now may be "murkier," which sounds negative, but leaves the impression that that's okay. The "top-down" way things were done in the past may have been more clean-cut and perhaps accomplished more, but "top-down" also has a negative connotation.

A similar opinion on a related issue was voiced earlier in an interview with David Nasby, vice president of the General Mills Foundation. "I refuse to lament the changes that have come with time," Nasby said. "I think the times today are so much more exciting than they were 20 years ago when all those wonderful things were said about Minnesota as the kind of social responsibility Mecca of the world."

Nasby describes the situation then as being paternalistic, with a very narrow band of Good Housekeeping Seal of Approval for organizations that had the resources. "I think there is much more discipline in philanthropy today than there has ever been before," he said.

In the earlier more paternalistic system, some had a tendency to just throw money at target problems and then felt absolved from responsibility, Nasby said, adding, "but it's not their money; it's the stockholders' money."

Nasby listed two tests: "What are the needs of the community, and how effective are the programs in meeting those needs? When you can answer those two questions," he said, "then I am not embarrassed to stand in front of stockholders and tell them that's how we used part of their money.

"A company is successful in direct proportion and relationship to the quality of the community in which it operates. That's something that was clearly articulated by the previous generation and sticks in the mind of the executive leadership."

In describing the operations of the General Mills Foundation, Nasby said, "We meet for two hours once a quarter. The agenda calls for spending one hour studying community problems and issues and then the second hour acting on grant requests. Invariably we spend at least an hour and a half on the first part of our agenda."

Nasby told of one member of the board who came to him and said, "You know, I'm supposed to help make decisions affecting the inner city. I've never lived in the inner city. What can I do to learn more?"

Nasby took him to various inner city projects to at least give him a beginning understanding of the situation. "Our executives take their responsibility seriously," Nasby said.

Others are not quite as sanguine. At least they want to raise some questions and make comparisons. But back to Neerland, who does so in a rather breezy style, and perhaps with tongue partially in cheek at times.

"Here's how we used to do things," says Neerland. "Sometime in the mid 1970s—I forget what the issue was, probably something to do with downtown housing—I remember some city official and I were complaining to Peter Gillette, then executive this-or-that for Northwestern National Bank. (At various times he had been chair of the Minneapolis bank and vice chairman of its holding company.)

"Our lament was that First National Bank wasn't on board. We were talking on the skyway level of the old Northwestern National Bank, and Gillette said he'd go and call on Jim Hetland, an executive of First Bank, and see what the heck was going on.

"And off he ran—and I mean he ran—across the skyway toward the Cargill Building. Shortly thereafter, First Bank joined the cause. None of us thought it was odd that the world worked this way." That's the way things were done then. A more sedate—though equally informal technique—was the proverbial private meeting of CEOs at the Minneapolis Club.

How did Gillette and Hetland get such power that they could make high-level decisions without having to clear it with a half dozen committees, or even their own CEOs? They had sterling civic and political credentials as well as corporate standing. They had been members of the Metropolitan Council not too many years earlier. Hetland had been its chair.

Other prominent corporate and first family figures served on the Council—Donald Dayton and Dennis Dunne to name just two.

"Name two today, if you can," says Neerland, with the assumption that it would be difficult to do so. "In those days civic enterprise was seen through this public-service public-good prism. Businesses were run to some extent by people who had been trained in the arts and culture of politics, service and business. It was the Minneapolis way." CEOs played an active role and held positions of leadership in civic organizations. Because most of these companies are global today, their CEOs spend much of their time out of the country, or at least in other parts of the United States, away from their headquarters community.

Increasingly corporate management became professionalized. Business school-trained people were brought in. They might or might not have any particular understanding of the community, let alone ties or loyalties to the local culture.

Some people ask the question, "What was so bad about the 'good old days' when you didn't have to go through a battery of vice presidents before you could get a decision, when a dozen men—and in those days there were virtually all men, mostly CEOs of corporations—would gather for breakfast or lunch at the Minneapolis Club and commit their corporations to several million or more dollars in support of a project?"

During the construction and later modernization of the Nicollet Mall in Minneapolis, John McHugh, then president of Northwestern National Bank, devoted virtually full time to the project. Call it paternalism if you will, or top-down management, but at least you got something done, which according to some people was more than is happening today. Isn't it better to have something clean-cut and have it be successful than for the sake of the political correctness of the day succumb to murkiness that goes under the name of democracy, and whose effectiveness is dubious?

"By the 1990s," Neerland says, "the corporate leaders of the community had isolated themselves in the Minnesota Business Partnership, a worthy organization, but one whose perspective was statewide and concentrated almost exclusively on direct business."

But in the final analysis, Neerland comes down in favor of murkiness as the greater potential. "We have a perhaps more democratic and less top-down form of civic enterprise emerging," he says. "Its outlines are murky, but I think that some of the younger (under 50) corporate executives are willing to take their turn in finding ways to consider issues and rally behind them. The [Citizens] League should be able to play an important role with this new breed. The Minneapolis Downtown Council is redefining a role for itself as well. I hope these signs point to a renewal of vigorous civic enterprise."

Another organization poised to play a leading role is the Minnesota Center for Corporate Responsibility. One of its challenges will be to enroll the younger executives in active membership, giving them freedom to devise plans and programs of their own.

Ken Dayton once said, "One of the reasons our city has been so successful is that we hire people of real ability and then turn them loose without feeling that we have to look over their shoulder all the time.

As reported in Chapter 1, one relatively new CEO said bluntly, "The constant reminder that we're not as good as our forerunners will be a self-fulfilling prophecy if people aren't careful. I really resent it. We are no less committed to society than our predecessors were. But at this rate, we may not be given the chance to demonstrate it."

So, are partnerships still being formed, and are they as strong as they were in the 1960s, or is there an erosion of that spirit?

Let's look at a couple of developments in St. Paul—30 years apart—and see how the present compares with the past.

Capital Centre project in St. Paul in the 1960s is a classic example of high-level business involvement in urban and community affairs. But so is a current project during the 1990s.

"To the casual observer," said Robert Van Hoef, vice president of First National Bank in St. Paul during the 1960s and 1970s, "there wasn't really anything drastically wrong with St. Paul at the start of the 1960s. It remained a pleasant, conservative and comfortable community. In general, St. Paul appeared to be satisfied being just what it was with no intention of changing.

"But things were happening elsewhere and so, to stay in step with progress, the city commissioned several outside planners to do some visionary planning for St. Paul's future. The resultant plans did two things—enlarged on the appreciation of things as they were, and generated some local controversy over proposals. No action resulted.

"What we are doing here in St. Paul," Van Hoef told the city's Rotary Club, "is a part of the most pressing domestic issue facing our country. It is the search for *The Great American City*—the other side of the coin of the often publicized *Urban Problem*."

Finally, in 1961, it was the peak of frustration that forced business and labor leaders to join hands with city officials to initiate some kind of rebuilding program. Forty-five top-level executives from business, labor and industry formed the Metropolitan Improvement Committee with the common commitment to apply their individual and corporate resources to a community redevelopment program.

Typical of the way things were done in St. Paul then, Philip Nason, president of First National Bank, assigned vice president Van Hoef to devote virtually full time as executive vice president of the Metropolitan Improvement Committee.

"With considerable courage," says Van Hoef, "the core of downtown St. Paul was marked for redevelopment. Instead of relying on outside experts to tell us what we ought to do, we turned to four civic-minded local architectural firms who banded together to produce the designs and ideas for a new central business district to be called Capital Centre."

The project covered some 12 blocks, involving approximately $26 million in property acquisition and clearance plus several hundred million dollars for a Dayton's department store, Hilton Hotel, a telephone company headquarters building and a Toni Company expansion project.

"Building cities is a combination of public and private effort," says Van Hoef. "Today as never before, the economic feasibility of large-scale community building relies on a close cooperation between public and private interests."

All of this happened in the 1960s in a period of outstanding partner relationships. That's 30 years ago. Cities deteriorate. They need upkeep. And the population grows. So in the 1990s that started happening in St. Paul too. How is the problem being solved today? A virtual replay of the 1960s.

Again the business community took the lead, this time under the leadership of Mayor Norman Coleman and Douglas Leatherdale, CEO of The St. Paul Companies, one of the nation's leading insurance companies. He was the founder in 1996 of the Capital City Partnership and the chairman of its 45-member board of directors, most of them CEOs. Twenty-five companies pledged $25,000 each to analyze the needs of the city as a first step toward pulling St. Paul out of a slump.

John Labosky was named president of Capital City Partnership, which is now in its third year. Ten years ago he held a similar position in Minneapolis, helping that city to successfully revitalize its downtown business area. Now he was being asked to help St. Paul do the same thing.

"If you had told me in 1996 that by 1998 we would have 45 member companies in St. Paul, each contributing $25,000 a year, I would have felt that you had lost your senses. But that is precisely what has happened," said Labosky.

The approaches of Capital Centre more than 30 years ago and Capital City Partnership today are similar. Both have resulted in massive building programs in downtown St. Paul.

But they have two major differences. The companies involved in the 1960s Capital Centre wanted their city to survive and thrive, and thrive it did. Their main emphasis was on buildings. Obviously buildings alone don't make a city, no matter how striking their architecture may be.

The assignment for Capital City Partnership was to be a planning group, to help the city understand what it was that the city really needed to provide a high quality of life. Perhaps parks were just as important as buildings. Perhaps they could be patterned after some European cities where people gather in small communities. Entertainment and a lively night life was also important.

Another major difference between Capital Centre and Capital City Partnership was the financial investment and involvement of numerous large Minneapolis corporations in the success of the St. Paul project.

"Do you know of any other place in the country where corporations of one city have been so involved in the development of another city?" Labosky asked.

Capital City Partnership gives a new meaning to partnership, and thus a new appreciation of how two cities often viewed as rivals can work together. That's a new contribution of the Minnesota Legacy. The reappraisal passes the test.

Chapter 13

WHERE DO WE GO FROM HERE?

To use the metaphor of a track meet: the runners brace one foot against the starting block behind them, from which they push off as they spring forward. The annual meeting of the Greater Minneapolis Chamber of Commerce on November 12, 1997, becomes such a jumping off point for this final chapter.

That meeting served a two-fold purpose. It honored the Carlson Companies as the first recipient of the Minnesota Keystone Program Honored Company Award—the Keystone's highest honor—for its longstanding commitment to the community, and it paid special tribute to the Minnesota Keystone Program℠ for its 50 years of philanthropy.

Appropriately, the speaker for the event was Marilyn Carlson Nelson, daughter of Curt Carlson, founder of the Carlson Companies.

In several ways her speech was an excellent bridge between the past and the future. First of all, there is the Curt Carlson story itself, starting 60 years ago with $50 of borrowed money and turning it into a company with $31 billion in annual sales under its various brands. A true example of Minnesota entrepreneurship.

It's also the story of turning over the company to a new generation of leadership, all the more significant because within a year Marilyn Carlson Nelson herself was named CEO of the company, adding to the much too slowly growing list of women in CEO positions in large corporations.

"Metaphorically speaking," said Nelson, "we are here today to talk about the transfer of a precious heirloom from one generation to another, a precious heirloom handed down to us by those who went before: our community.

"For many of you younger people in the room, this will have to be a history lesson. In the post-Kennedy era, there was a different attitude in the country, a feeling that the government could and should do many, many things for the citizenry.

"The federal government made money available through huge block grants to the states, which, in turn, passed them on to local communities. The rationale was that community leaders could and should know how to spend tax dollars to build our own cities.

"Minnesota took a different approach," said Nelson. "Our businesses opted not to retreat and let the federal, state or municipal governments handle the load. But at the same time we did not simply pass the responsibility back to the individuals either. Our corporations stunned the nation by actually contributing five percent of pre-tax income. Remember, at the time the national average was less than one percent."

It's not for naught that Dun and Bradstreet calls Minnesota "one of the strongest economic areas in the U.S." or that *SAVVY* Magazine credits Minnesota as "the best place for raising children in the country."

"At the Carlson Company we have always believed that our future depended on an even-handed approach to shareholders, customers, employees, suppliers and the community," said Nelson. "Enlightened shareholder value will, I believe, move corporations back to a more responsible, responsive role in the lives of our people and our communities."

Nelson called for humility in taking credit for our healthy economy and community. "Those of us in my generation have drunk from wells we did not dig," she said.

William McDonough, dean of the school of architecture at the University of Virginia, spoke on a similar subject on January 8, 1998, as part of the Landmark Series Public Affairs Forum in St. Paul. The forum was jointly sponsored by the Minnesota Center for Corporate Responsibility, the Upper Midwest Chapter of Business for Social Responsibility, and the Landmark Center, with financial assistance from the business community.

Following up his address in a column in the *Star Tribune,* McDonough said, "Our children will benefit—and we will benefit—if we design a future grounded in principles of economic, environmental and social sustainability."

Pointing out that our children will measure progress by our legacy, not our activity, McDonough said, "We often think we are measuring progress and prosperity when we are only talking about economic activity. When the *Exxon Valdez* goes down in Prince William Sound, economic indicators like Gross Domestic Product go up. We're measuring activity."

"With our present strategy, the legacy we are leaving our children," said McDonough, are "sprawls, with their economic, environmental and social costs; toxic human-made chemicals, hundreds of them, now endemic in the environment; plant and animal species destroyed, their irreplaceable beauty and genetic information lost. Our quality of life can be better and our economy more sustaining if we innovate to eliminate the concept of waste and seek to free ourselves from regulation."

McDonough cited some examples of innovation: an American carpeting company now leases carpets it once sold, thereby releasing a billion-dollar asset. When the customer is done with it, the company recycles it into new carpeting.

"Our quality of life can be better," McDonough said, "if we design buildings and neighborhoods for the people who will live and work in them as well as for those who will construct them. In the process we can design systems that let people spend time with their families and lessen the load on the region's increasingly congested roadways."

When McDonough was asked, "How can you get people to adopt such seemingly far-out programs?" his one-word answer was "profit." In the long run, it's simply less costly and therefore more profitable to do things that way. What is right and what is profitable are not either-or choices.

Granted, there are some business people whose first concern is whether or not a venture is profitable. For something to be profitable does not automatically mean that it can't also be right. There is not all that much distinction between what is right and what is profitable if you begin to think long-term instead of short-term.

Danie Watson, president of The Watson Group, a communications consultant group in Wayzata, said, "In my eagerness to get corporations to think ethically, I used to start out by trying to encourage them to do certain things because they are right, and that they also happen to be profitable. I have changed my approach. I now begin by pointing out that a lot of things that are profitable also happen to be right. The two are not mutually exclusive."

This is the kind of long-range analysis and planning that appeals to communities like Minnesota and organizations like the Minnesota Center for Corporate Responsibility, Business for Social Responsibility and the Caux Round Table.

Some activities and programs are based on simple common sense. Not that they were whipped up in a hurry without regard for rigorous research, but rather with an attitude: "Of course we ought to do this. Why didn't we do it long ago? Let's do what it takes to get going."

One program in that category is MCCR's Work/Life Strategies. The project was designed by a 32-member task force, chaired by Clinton O. Larson, former corporate vice president of operations at Honeywell, Inc.

Work/Life policies and strategies are not new. For almost two decades many leading companies have struggled to help employees balance the competing responsibilities of work and family life. "It is time for companies to acknowledge the primacy of family in the value systems of both men and women," says Lawrence Perlman, president, chairman and CEO of Ceridian Corporation. "Too many women still have to choose between career and family. And too often men sacrifice participation in the lives of their families to meet the demands of their jobs. The cost to both people and the companies they work for are too high."

The MCCR Work/Life strategies already has had a good start. Its 52-page workbook, *Creating High Performance Organizations: The Bottom Line Value of Work/Life Strategies* is being used by corporations who are taking responsibility for the families of their employees seriously.

The future for MCCR itself is equally encouraging, both on the local scene and globally. It has become known for sponsoring or co-sponsoring a variety of workshops on business ethics and corporate responsibility, including such events as lectures by McDonough and other leading futurists.

It is often difficult to argue that two approaches to the solution for a problem are of equal importance, whether it be global versus local, or financial profits listed on the bottom line versus ample consideration for the welfare of people. It's like the chicken and the egg argument. Which comes first and, therefore, which is more important?

One could argue that the local emphasis is more important than the global, because without a strong local base there will be insufficient strength for going global. Conversely, without due attention to the global opportunities, the local base will wither away.

In the everyday business world, giving more emphasis to human welfare than to bottom line profits may eventually put a company out of existence altogether, thus really benefitting no one. On the other hand, squeezing
the work force to get the last penny for profit may eventually also do in both
the company and the workers.

It may not always require an exact fifty-fifty division, but if the spread
between the two forces gets too big, both with suffer.

A Twin Cities case in point: The H.B. Fuller Company has long been
recognized for being truly committed to the stakeholder concept of perhaps even giving slightly greater—or at least equal—priority to employees,
customers and the community rather than to shareholders. The company
philosophy has been that it is precisely because of this emphasis that the
company has been successful, and the shareholders have regularly received
their dividends.

However, even this company has had to recognize that perhaps the bottom financial line needed attention. And so for the first time in its 111-year
history, it has chosen a CEO from outside the company, Al Stroucken, of
Bayer AG in Germany.

According to the *Minneapolis Star Tribune* in spring 1998, H. B. Fuller
chairman Tony Andersen acknowledged the need for fast action which may
include closing or selling off some divisions that are not profitable, and pos-
sibly some layoffs. However, Andersen believes that the necessary corrections
can be made without harming Fuller's much-praised corporate culture.

Stroucken is not a "gunslinger," Andersen said. He is the opposite of
Chainsaw Al Dunlop, who earned his nickname by slashing jobs with aban-
don. Andersen said, "Stroucken is a quick study and a methodical analyzer
who is doing a marvelous job at working with Fuller managers to identify
problem areas and zero in on appropriate solutions.

The banking community in the Twin Cities provides another example
of differing approaches. Some of the major banks like the former First Bank

and Norwest have grown by mergers and acquisitions to become national in scope. Others, like Western and Riverside have adopted the concept of a community bank, concentrating on serving smaller communities with different needs.

MCCR can play a key role in promoting discussions that will bring out the best in various approaches.

As this manuscript is being prepared for publication, exciting plans are under way for a joint venture involving MCCR, the University of Minnesota Carlson School of Management and the University of St. Thomas Graduate School of Business.

The three partners will combine their talents and experience to assist business leaders in creating ethical and profitable business cultures at the enterprise, community and global levels.

The partners plan to expand business services, launch research projects on ethics and corporate citizenship, develop best practices, case research and enrich educational programs. The Center plans a special focus on global ethics management and will build on its existing *Business Ethics Network*SM and its *Work ↔ Life Network*SM. The Center will also focus on building business involvement in communities. As the Center re-invents itself for the future, the Board of Directors (reference Appendix 1) has chosen a new name for the organization—the Center for Ethical Business Cultures (CEBC) to be implemented in the first half of the Year 2000.

These various initiatives are intended to ask questions and to lead in a search for answers that are of critical importance to business leaders—such questions as can ethical business conduct be linked to profitability?

What are standards of ethical conduct on which business can agree that cut across cultural and national boundaries? What are new and effective ways of committing employees to high standards of ethics, responsibility and civic involvement? How can business lead most effectively in addressing community and social issues? What practical models work and how can they be adapted across cultures? How can research and scholarship inform business decision makers about ethical dimensions of critical issues like human rights, environmental sustainability, employee relations, the gap between rich and poor? What role can corporate directors play in overseeing the ethical dimensions of the corporation? How can business create an ethical organizational culture? What management processes are most effective? What training is most effective?

Similar questions are being raised in other parts of the world as well, and the Minnesota Center for Corporate Responsibility, through its relationship with the Caux Round Table, is helping to address them.

Books published in the last five years in the United States and Great Britain that have received particular acclaim include *The Future of Capitalism* by Lester Thurow, *The Rise of the Social Entrepreneur* by Charles Ledbetter, *When Corporations Rule the World* by David C. Korten, and *The Ecology of Commerce* by Paul Hawken.

Both Korten and Hawken are adept at painting the horrors of the present global problems. Hawken is more optimistic that something can be done about them and that it can and must be done by business itself. For starters, he points out eight objectives, the final one being to have some fun while doing it and strive for an aesthetic outcome. "The urge to create beauty," says Hawken, "is an untapped power, and it exists in commerce as well as in society."

Perhaps the most provocative recent writing on these subjects comes from the pen of the British writer, Charles Handy, in his 1998 book, *The Hungry Spirit.*

A few chapter headings will give you a quick insight into his trend of thinking. Under a section, "A Creaking Capitalism," Handy writes about such subjects as "The Limits of Markets: too much was expected of them; When Efficiency Is Ineffective: when too much of a good thing is bad; The Baby and the Bathwater: the essentials of capitalism."

Another section is titled "Towards a Decent Society," elaborated upon in such chapters as "A Better Capitalism: re-inventing capitalism"; "The Citizen Company: a different sort of business"; "A Part of Government: government as a servant."

In this day of globalization, Handy's insight is particularly helpful in pointing out that global emphasis does not totally supersede the local.

Handy writes, "Multinational companies have, perforce, become federal, although they don't always call it that or recognize what they have done. The need to be both local and global, or to be what some call multi-local, has forced them to work out a form of governance that gives as much authority to the local bodies as is possible without endangering the whole."

This recognition has implications for corporate CEOs who think that the demands on their time by the global justifies cutting down on their attention to its local headquarters community. Corporations will continue to have a special responsibility to all of the communities in which they operate.

But perhaps one of the best thought provokers in the whole book comes in the first two paragraphs of Chapter One. "In Africa, they say there are two kinds of hunger, the lesser hunger and the greater hunger. The lesser hunger is for the things that sustain life, the goods and services, and the money to pay for them, which we all need. The greater hunger is for an answer to the question 'why?' for some understanding of what that life is for.

"In the capitalist societies, however, it has been our comfortable assumption, so far, that we can best satisfy the greater hunger by appeasing the lesser hunger."

Actually, it is just the reverse. We do not solve the greater hunger by concentrating on solving more of the lesser hungers. The better we understand the greater hunger, the more likely will be to develop appropriate business plans and structures that will make for a better society.

The Minnesota Center for Corporate Responsibility is committed to helping the world understand that thesis.

END NOTE

As was stated in the preface ("A word from the author"), Honeywell, Inc., a long-time stalwart in Minneapolis, was bought by Allied Signal, whose headquarters are in New Jersey, as the manuscript of this book was going to press. Curt Johnson was asked by Minnesota Public Radio to evaluate the implications of this move. Johnson has held various high level positions in Minnesota as head of the Citizen's League, the Metropolitan Council and a chief of staff for Governor Arne Carlson.

"There is no question about this being a blow," Johnson says. "In the near term the loss is greatest to community leadership. Honeywell has been the driving force around a new seriousness to make the Phillips neighborhood of south Minneapolis safe, to restore housing opportunities and create jobs.

"But all the hand-wringing over the loss of a headquarters seems to inspire questions about how did this happen? Could we have prevented this decision? Whose fault is it, losing yet another headquarters?"

But these are probably the wrong questions, Johnson says. Furthermore, he warns that "in the face of relentless globalization penetrating the strategies and decisions of nearly every enterprise, we should expect to lose most of these headquarters in the next generation. Bad luck in some ways, just like the good luck that brought them to us in the past."

And then he provides some challenging advice. "Instead of cramming our desperate fingers into the dike," he says, "we ought to ponder a new set of questions."

Has the time come, he asks, "when this region, after a couple of generations of harvesting the good ideas of the families who founded our largest firms, should build a strategy for sustainable economic success that fits the new realities and rules of the globalized age?"

We never needed a strategy before, but we do now, Johnson said.

Part of that strategy might well be to give a greater attention to who our community leaders will be in the future. In our reliance on the strong leadership of the past, mostly of Anglo-Saxon background, we have overlooked another sizable group of current as well as potential leaders, both in age and in ethnic backgrounds. They are there and they are increasingly coming to the fore. Several of them have been touched on in this book. They may be in the minority now, but whoever writes a book on this subject in the future will find them in large numbers.

"Now we should examine what our comparative advantages are," Johnson urges. "What industry clusters have emerged that appear strong? Which do we want to build on? Is our public policy framework with its regulations and investments tuned to these emerging opportunities (or, on closer examination, guilty of propping up what's left of the old arrangements)? With quality of life fast becoming a piece of the bottom line for location decisions—are we paying the right attention to the currency of our infrastructure—the old kind and the new kind? Are we planning to preserve mobility, community safety, good neighborhoods, our natural resources such as the lakes and parks? Are we serious about improving education for kids, in view of likely chronic shortages in the work force?"

In other words, the past can teach us some lessons. Let's not endanger ourselves by letting them hide the lessons we need to learn about how to deal with the future. Learning from the great heritage of the past, today's younger generations face the challenge of a different future.

EPILOGUE

By James W. Renier, chairman
Board of Directors
Minnesota Center for Corporate Responsibility

T he book you have just read is a history. It is a history of values, ethics and responsibility. It presents stated convictions of business leaders and a lot of anecdotal evidence that should provide the reader with insights into the culture of Minnesota business. Its importance is that this group of philosophies and actions form a legacy upon which one can continue to build.

It is a legacy of ethics and community involvement and a belief that these are important to good business. The record speaks for itself—Minnesota business and corporate responsibility are thought of everywhere when either one or the other is mentioned.

I have been very involved with the Minnesota Center for Corporate Responsibility (as its chairman for the last four years) and the Minnesota Business Partnership (as a member of the executive committee and its education subcommittee chairman for five years). Upon reading the manuscript of this book, I obtained a new appreciation of a factor that motivated my own actions while engaged in these activities. It especially helped me understand the passion for children's education that occurred during my tenure at Honeywell and the last five years as a retired CEO.

I am often asked why I continue to have such an interest in education and kids, which seems almost like "flunking" retirement. I usually respond with statements about morality and responsibility.

As I raised a number of kids as a single parent, I learned about children and schools. For forty years I worked for a company and with an executive group that believed in being completely ethical, and I felt responsible to collaborate with the community to solve community problems. The conviction was always there that this simply was good for business and the right thing to do; and it was done even on a global basis. That conviction did not come to an end at retirement. Just the opposite. The forty years spent in business could now be used in a much more intensive way to help children succeed.

Many studies and myriad surveys indicate that a lack of morality, questionable ethics, violence, school dropouts, abused children, drugs, etc., present many more challenges than in the past; and the costs in taxes, medical charges, family strife, employee morale, lost productivity, etc., has greatly increased.

Is there really any doubt that we'll need more, not less, of what business can bring to the party to solve these problems and prevent them from hurting business and the economy? Which businesses will win in the long run, those that deal with the reality or those that delegate the problems? Is there a more compelling issue for business success in the future than the health, education and responsible behavior of kids?

With all the mothers in the work force, what about work and family stability? My last ten years of hands-on experience tell me that the solution to these problems need the time and talent of top-level business people more than ever before. Without this business leadership involving not just money, but time and talent, we will not progress. The public sector and the not-for-profits cannot get the job done without the leadership and skills of business people. One could indeed become depressed. Many of the solutions elude the bureaucracies and always seem to require more resources. Business people, however, have found that solutions to many of the problems do not require rocket science. Plenty of resources exist if it is possible to identify barriers and creatively eliminate them through the use of a heavy dose of collaboration and common sense.

The legacy spoken of earlier is not just one of interest in leadership, but also in common sense. To succeed requires responsibility, passion and influence at the CEO levels. It is a legacy of action at the highest levels and involvement, not reliance on the constant repetition of fourth order ideological principles with simplistic one-liners for others to apply. Bureaucratic barrier removal and community asset development are required. The practical sense and the integrity of the businessman must trump the politics.

Traditional business has always lobbied for lower taxes and reduced spending. Given the propensities to spend, this action will probably continue. But as stated in this book, past business leaders in Minnesota were involved in far more than lobbying for lower taxes and reduced spending. They also led the charge for being involved in community issues that ultimately affected not only the quality of local business, but also the general quality of life for the community itself. They recognized correctly that bureaucracies alone cannot get the job done, and that left to their own they just become more numerous and much larger.

The cynics feel that corporate responsibility is just another social distraction from the bottom line. If needed, they believe, one can go to a graduate school to learn about the business of "corporate responsibility." Based on my work with children, I have concluded that graduate schools, including schools of education, need to do a much better job at understanding the role of business in leveraging positive change in business and in our society.

The Minnesota legacy is timely, relevant and responsible. It is good to record the rich history of those business people that created the Minnesota Business Partnership and The Minnesota Center for Corporate Responsibility. Perhaps it will help redouble our resolve. Perhaps it will cause more of our business leaders to build upon a globally admired legacy.

We can be thankful for the legacy that we have been given and for all that it has accomplished. We must built on it or our business itself will feel the pain of corporate neglect.

Appendix I

MCCR BOARD OF DIRECTORS, 1998-1999

Officers

Chairman
James J. Renier, Ph.D.
Retired Chairman & CEO
Honeywell Inc.

Treasurer
Michael J. Evers, Ph.D.
Dean Emeritus
Graduate School of Business
University of St. Thomas

Secretary
Thomas E. Holloran, J.D.
Professor
MBA Director, Management
Graduate School of Business
University of St. Thomas

Directors

Anthony L. Andersen
Chair, Board of Directors
H.B. Fuller Company

Catherine A. Anderson
President & CEO
e-med.OnCall, Inc.

David L. Andreas
President & CEO
National City Bancorporation

Paul Baszucki
Chairman & CEO
Norstan, Inc.

Norman E. Bowie, Ph.D.
Executive Vice President of Seminars
Aspen Institute

James R. Campbell
Chairman, President and CEO
Norwest Bank Minnesota, N.A.

John F. Carlson
Former Chairman & CEO
Cray Research, Inc.

John W. Castro
President & CEO
Merrill Corporation

Judith S. Corson
Partner & Co-founder
Customs Research Inc.

William H. Ellis
Retired President & CEO
Piper Capital Management

Theodore L. Fredrickson, Ph.D.
Dean
Graduate School of Business
University of St. Thomas

Kenneth E. Goodpaster, Ph.D.
Professor
Koch Chair in Business Ethics
Graduate School of Business
University of St. Thomas

Esperanza Guerrero-Anderson
President & CEO
Milestone Growth Fund, Inc.

George C. Halvorson
President & CEO
HealthPartners, Inc.

James L. Hetland, Jr.
Rtd. Sr. Vice President & General Counsel
First Bank, N.A.

Ronald N. Hoge
President & CEO
MagneTek, Inc.

James J. Howard
Chairman, President & CEO
Northern States Power Company

David S. Kidwell, Ph.D.
Dean
Carlson School of Management
University of Minnesota

David A. Koch
Chairman of the Board
Graco, Inc.

Richard G. Lareau, J.D.
Partner
Oppenheimer Wolff & Donnelly

Clinton O. Larson
Corporate Vice President Operations, Retired
Honeywell Inc.

Robert W. MacGregor
President
MN Center for Corporate Responsibility

Richard D. McFarland
Vice Chairman
Dain Rauscher Corporation

Hazel R. O'Leary
Honorary Member
Former Secretary of Energy, U.S.A.

Roger Parkinson
Publisher & Chief Executive
The Globe and Mail

Galen T. Pate
Chairman
United Community Bancshares

James P. Shannon
Rtd. Vice President & Executive Director
General Mills Foundation

John G. Turner
Chairman & CEO
ReliaStar Financial Corp.

Donald C. Wegmiller
President
MCG/HealthCare Compensation

Appendix 2

SPRING HILL CONFERENCE PARTICIPANTS NOVEMBER 15 AND 16, 1977

Anthony L. Andersen
President and CEO
H. B. Fuller Company

DeWalt H. Ankeny, Jr.
President and Chief Executive Officer
First National Bank of Minneapolis

Edward W. Asplin
Vice Chairman and Chief Administrative
    Officer
Bemis Company

Judson Bemis
Chairman of Executive Committee
Bemis Company

Coleman Bloomfield
President and Chairman
Minnesota Mutual Life Insurance Com-
    pany

Jerry V. Catt
Public Affairs
Jostens

John Cowles, Jr.
Chairman
Minneapolis Star Tribune

Jack J. Crocker
Chairman and Chief Executive Officer
SuperValu Stores

Harry P. Day
President
Spring Hill Center

Bruce B. Dayton

Kenneth N. Dayton
Chairman
Dayton Hudson Corporation

H. Robert Diercks
Vice Chairman
Cargil

Herbert H. Dow
Chairman
Public Interest Company
The Dow Center

C. B. Drake, Jr.
President and Chairman
St Paul Companies

Donald R. Dwight
Publisher
Minneapolis Star Tribune

William George
President
Litton Microwave Cooking Products

E. Peter Gillette, Jr.
Executive Vice President
Northwestern National Bank of Min-
    neapolis

N. Bud Grossman
Chairman and President
Gelco Corporation

Roger L. Hale
President and Chief Executive Officer
Tennant Company

William A. Hodder
President
Donaldson Company

Thomas E. Holloran
Chairman and President
Inter-Regional Financial Group

John Hulse
Vice President and CEO for Minnesota
    Northwestern
Bell Telephone Company

Geri Joseph
Contributing Editor
Minneapolis Tribune

E. Robert Kinney
Chairman and CEO
General Mills

David A. Koch
President
Graco

Charles Krusell
Executive Vice President
Minneapolis Chamber of Commerce

Sylvester Laskin
Chairman and CEO
Minnesota Power and Light Company

Donald W. McCarthy
President and CEO
Northern States Power Company

David T. McLaughlin
Chairman and CEO
Toro Company

Louis W. Menk
Chairman and CEO
Burlington Northern

John W. Morrison
Chairman and CEO
Northwestern National Bank of Min-
    neapolis

Leonard H. Murray
President
Soo Line Railroad Company

William C. Norris
Chairman and CEO
Control Data Corporation

Dale R. Olseth
President and CEO
Medtronic

John Pearson
President
Northwestern National Life Insurance
  Company

William G. Phillips
Chairman and CEO
International Mutlifoods Corporation

Harry C. Piper, Jr.
President
Piper, Jaffray, Hopwood

Stephen L. Pistner
Executive Vice President
Dayton Hudson Corporation

Charles W. Poe, Jr.
President
Metropolitan Economic Development

Glendora M. Putnam
Equal Opportunity Officer
Massachusetts Housing Finance Agency

Gary B. Rappaport
Chairman and CEO
Napco Industries

Gerald Rauenhorst
President
Rauenhorst Corporation

Henry B. Schacht
Chairman and CEO
Cummins Engine Company

James P. Shannon
Executive Director
The Minneapolis Foundation

Richard O. Simpson
President
Richard Simpson Associates

David Sirota
President
David Sirota Associates

G. Richard Slade
President
Northwestern National Bank of St. Paul

Ronald K. Speed
Director
Corporate Community Relations
Honeywell

Edson W. Spencer
President and CEO
Honeywell

William H. Spoor
Chairman and CEO
The Pillsbury Company

Richard H. Vaughan
President
Northwestern Bancorporation

Winston R. Wallin
President and CEO
The Pillsbury Company

Frederick T. Weyerhaeuser
President
Conwed Corporation

Mark H. Willes
President
Federal Reserve Bank

C. Angus Wurtele
Chairman and CEO
Valspar Corporation

Thomas H. Wyman
President and CEO
Green Giant Company

Appendix 3

Minnesota Keystone Program[SM]
1998 Membership List

1998 Keystone Five Percent Participants

Adolfson & Peterson Construction
Albrechts Furs
Allina Health System
Alternative Staffing, Inc.
American Business Forms, Inc.
Andersen Consulting
Anonymous Participant
Beacon Bank
BlueCross BlueShield of Minnesota
*Bolger Publications/Creative Printing
Braun Intertec Corporation
Bremer Bank Brekenridge
Bremer of Alexandria
Bremer of Brainerd
Bremer Trust
Briggs and Morgan, Professional Association
The Brimeyer Group, Inc.
Bursch Travel Agency, Inc.
C.J. Olson Market Research, Inc.

Caliber Development Corporation
*Carlson Companies, Inc.
Carmichael Lynch, Inc.
Catalog Marketing Services (CMS)
Cincinnatus Inc.
Cinequipt, Inc.
Citizens State Bank of Tyler, Inc.
Citizens State Bank of Waverly
Clarity Coverdale Fury Advertising, Inc.
Commercial Furniture Services, Inc.
Anonymous Participant
Anonymous Participant
Custom Communications, Inc.
*Dain Rauscher
*Dayton Hudson Corporation
Deloitte & Touche LLp
Donlar Construction Company
dor and associates, inc.
Dorsey & Whitney L.L.P.
Driessen Water

155

Eller Media Company
Faegre & Benson LLP
Faribault Woolen Mill Company
Farmers State Bank of Hamel
Fingerhut Companies, Inc.
The First National Bank in Cannon Falls
First Security Bank—Lake Benton
· Fluoroware, Inc.
Foldcraft Co.
Foster Klima & Company
Fountain Industries Company
Future Focus
*Gabberts Furniture and Design Studio
Gage Marketing Group
Gold'n Plump Poultry
Goodall Manufacturing Company
Gopher Sport
Grant & Palombo Marketing Services Inc.
Grant Thornton LLP
Gray, Plant, Mooty, Mooty & Bennett, P.A.
Hanft Fride
*The Hartfiel Company
Health Partners
HealthEast Care System
Himle Horner, Inc.
Holden Graphic Services
HomeStyles Publishing and Marketing, Inc.
Hoye Home Furnishings & Appliance
Impact Mailing, Inc.
Interior Resources
J & B Equipment Company, Inc.
Jeane Thorne Inc.
Johnson Insurance Consultants
KARE 11 Television
PMG Peat Marwick LLP - Minneapolis
KTTC Television
Karlsson Consulting Group, Inc.
The Keewaydin Group, Inc.
Kerker Marketing Communications
Kopp Investment Advisors, Inc.
Leadership Foundations
Leather Center
Leslie J. Kraus & Associates, Inc.
Lieberman Companies, Inc.
Lighthouse Inc.
Lindsay Windows and Doors
Little & Company

Lone Oak Mailing and Fulfillment Services (LLC)
MSI Insurance
M.A. Mortenson Company
Mackay & Associates
*Mackay Envelope Corporation
The Maguire Agency
Mahoney Ulbrich Christiansen & Russ, P.A.
Markman Capital Management
Mars Company
Martin/Williams Advertising
Mary, Inc.
McGough Construction
Michaud Cooley Erickson
Midwest of Cannon Falls, Inc.
Minneapolis Home and Garden Show
Minnesota Timberwolves/Minnesota Lynx
Minnesota Wild
Minnesota Wire & Cable Co.
National Purity, Inc.
Nelson, Tietz & Hoye
Neuger Henry Bartkowski Public Relations
Neville & Associates
North Memorial Health Care
North Star Technical Resources, Inc.
Northeast Bank
Northwestern Foods, Inc.
*Opus Northwest, L.L.C.
Owens Services Corporation
Padilla Speer Beardsley Inc.
Park State Bank
Anonymous Participant
Performark, Inc.
Pine & Partners, Inc.
Preferred Adventures Ltd.
PricewaterhouseCoopers LLP
The Prouty Project
Public Strategies Group (PSG), The
RSP Architects, Ltd.
Anonymous Participant
Reell Precision Manufacturing Corporation
Rural Cellular Corporation
Rusten Marketing Group, Inc.

Sathe & Associates
Scherer Brothers Lumber Company
Shandwick International
Anonymous Participant
Silha Associates
Slumberland, Inc.
Anonymous Participant
Spangler Design Team
Staff-Plus, Inc.
Standard Heating & Air Conditioning
*Star Tribune
Stearnswood, Inc.
Stuart Management Corporation
Summit Mortgage Group
The TAPEMARK Company

The Thunderbird Hotel and Convention
  Center
Tom and Ann Wald Realty
Total Solutions Group
Tower Asphalt, Inc.
Town & Country State Bank of Winona
Anonymous Participant
Tunheim Santrizos
Vision Technologies
W.L. Hall Company
The Watson Group
Wild Rumpus
Wilkerson, Guthmann & Johnson, Ltd.
Williams Steel & Hardware Company
Yamamoto Moss
Ziegler Inc.

1998 Keystone Two Percent Participants

ADC Telecommunications, Inc.
Allied Companies LLC
Aon Risk Services, Inc. of Minnesota
*Arthur Andersen LLP
Bachman's, Inc.
Barrett Moving & Storage Company
Anonymous Participant
BFI of Minnesota, Inc.
BORN Information Services, Inc.
Bremer Bank of Willmar
Bremer Bank Southwest
Campbell Mithun Esty, L.L.C.
Cargill
Carl Bolander & Sons Co./SKB Environ-
  mental, Inc.
Colonial Craft
Commonwealth Electric of Minnesota,
  Inc.
Community National Bank in Northfield
Computer World, Inc.
Continental Press, Inc.
Deluxe Corporation
Doherty, Rumble & Butler, P.A.
Dolphin Staffing
Donaldson Company, Inc.
EMC Corporation
Edina Realty Home Services, Inc.
Ellerbe Becket

F & M Community Bank
First National Bank of Milaca
First State Bank of Wyoming
Franklin National Bank of Minneapolis
Fredrikson & Byron, P.A.
Gemini Incorporated
General Mills, Inc.
General Office Products Company
The Goodhue County National Bank
*Graco Inc.
Granite Falls Bank
*H.B. Fuller Company
Homecrest Industries Incorporated
Honeywell Inc.
Horton, Inc.
Johnson Consulting Services
Land O'Lakes, Inc.
Leonard, Street and Deinard
Lindquist & Vennum P.L.L.P.
Lyman Lumber Company & Affiliates
MDA Consulting Group, Inc.
Marco Business Products, Inc.
Marquette Bancshares, Inc.
Mason Brothers Company
*Medtronic, Inc.
The Merchants National Bank of Winona
Minnesota Mutual Companies
National City Bancorporation

Norstan, Inc.
North Shore Bank of Commerce
Northern States Power Company
Northwest Airlines
*Norwest Bank Minnesota
Oppenheimer Wolff & Donnelly
Pentair, Inc.
Pilgrim DryCleaners Inc.
The Pillsbury Company
Red Wing Shoe Company, Inc.
Reliant Energy Minnegasco
ReliaStar Financial Corp.
Remmele Engineering, Inc.
The Resource Companies
St. Anthony Park Bank
The St. Paul Companies
Saint Paul Pioneer Press
Security State Bank of Bemidji
Signal Bank
Smyth Companies
Stahl Construction Company

State Farm Insurance Companies
Stirtz Bernards Boyden Surdel & Larter, P.A.
Swanson & Youngdale, Inc.
Synet Service Corporation
TCF National Bank Minnesota
The Tegra Group, Inc.
Tennant Company
The Toro Company
Towle Real Estate Company
U.S. Bancorp
Union Bank & Trust
University National Bank of St. Paul
Upper Midwest Industries, Inc.
Viking Electric Supply, Inc.
The Voyageur Asset Management LLC
W.A. Lang Co.
Weeres Industries Corporation
Western Bank
Winona Knitting Mills, Div. of Hampshire Designers, Inc.

1998 Keystone Pledge Participants

A Plus Advertising Corp.

State Bank of Kimball

*There were 23 participating companies when the Minnesota Keystone Program was founded in 1976. Of the original group, 14 remain in the program today.

Appendix 4

CAUX ROUND TABLE
PRINCIPLES FOR BUSINESS

Introduction

The Caux Round Table believes that the world business community should play an important role in improving economic and social conditions. As a statement of aspirations, this document aims to express a world standard against which business behavior can be measured. We seek to begin a process that identifies shared values, reconciles differing values, and thereby develops a shared perspective on business behavior acceptable to and honored by all.

These principles are rooted in two basic ethical ideals: kyosei and human dignity. The Japanese concept of kyosei means living and working together for the common good enabling cooperation and mutual prosperity to coexist with healthy and fair competition. "Human dignity" refers to the sacredness or value of each person as an end, not simply as a mean to the fulfillment of others' purposes or even majority prescription.

The General Principles in Section 2 seek to clarify the spirit of kyosei and "human dignity," while the specific Stakeholder Principles in Section 3 are concerned with their practical application.

In its language and form, the document owes a substantial debt to *The Minnesota Principles,* a statement of business behavior developed by the Minnesota Center for Corporate Responsibility. The Center hosted and chaired the drafting committee, which included Japanese, European, and United States representatives.

Business behavior can affect relationships among nations and the prosperity and well-being of us all. Business is often the first contact between nations and, by the way in which it causes social and economic changes, has a significant impact on the level of fear or confidence felt by people worldwide. Members of the Caux Round Table place their first emphasis on putting one's own house in order, and on seeking to establish what is right rather than who is right.

Section I. Preamble

The mobility of employment, capital, products and technology is making business increasingly global in its transactions and its effects.

Law and market forces are necessary but insufficient guides for conduct.

Responsibility for the policies and actions of business and respect for the dignity and interests of its stakeholders are fundamental.

Shared values, including a commitment to shared prosperity, are as important for a global community as for communities of smaller scale.

For these reasons, and because business can be a powerful agent of positive social change, we offer the following principles as a foundation for dialogue and action by business leaders in search of business responsibility. In so doing, we affirm the necessity for moral values in business decision making. Without them, stable business relationships and a sustainable world community are impossible.

Section 2. General Principles

Principle 1. The Responsibilities of Businesses:
Beyond Shareholders toward Stakeholders

The value of a business to society is the wealth and employment it creates and the marketable products and services it provides to consumers at a reasonable price commensurate with quality. To create such value, a business must maintain its own economic health and viability, but survival is not a sufficient goal.

Businesses have a role to play in improving the lives of all their customers, employees, and shareholders by sharing with them the wealth they have created. Suppliers and competitors as well should expect businesses to honor their obligations in a spirit of honesty and fairness. As responsible citizens of the local, national, regional and global communities in which they operate, businesses share a part in shaping the future of those communities.

Principle 2. The Economic and Social Impact of Business:
Toward Innovation, Justice and World Community

Businesses established in foreign countries to develop, produce or sell should also contribute to the social advancement of those countries by creating productive employment and helping to raise the purchasing power of their citizens. Businesses also should contribute to human rights, education, welfare, and vitalization of the countries in which they operate. Businesses should contribute to economic and social development not only in the countries in which they operate, but also in the world community at large, through effective and prudent use of resources, free and fair competition, and emphasis upon innovation in technology, production methods, marketing and communications.

Principle 3. Business Behavior:
Beyond the Letter of Law Toward a Spirit of Trust

While accepting the legitimacy of trade secrets, businesses should recognize that sincerity, candor, truthfulness, the keeping of promises, and transparency contribute not only to their own credibility and stability but also to the smoothness and efficiency of business transactions, particularly on the international level.

Principle 4. Respect for Rules

To avoid trade frictions and to promote freer trade, equal conditions for competition, and fair and equitable treatment for all participants, businesses should respect international and domestic rules. In addition, they should recognize that some behavior, although legal, may still have adverse consequences.

Principle 5. Support for Multilateral Trade

Businesses should support the multilateral trade systems of the GATT/World Trade Organization and similar international agreements. They should cooperate in efforts to promote the progressive and judicious liberalization of trade and to relax those domestic measures that unreasonably hinder global commerce, while giving due respect to national policy objectives.

Principle 6. Respect for the Environment

A business should protect and, where possible, improve the environment, promote sustainable development, and prevent the wasteful use of natural resources.

Principle 7. Avoidance of Illicit Operations

A business should not participate in or condone bribery, money laundering, or other corrupt practices: indeed, it should seek cooperation with others to eliminate them. It should not trade in arms or other materials used for terrorist activities, drug traffic or other organized crime.

Section 3. Stakeholder Principles

Customers

We believe in treating all customers with dignity, irrespective of whether they purchase our products and services directly from us or otherwise acquire them in the market. We therefore have a responsibility to:

- provide our customers with the highest quality products and services consistent with their requirements;

- treat our customers fairly in all aspects of our business transactions, including a high level of service and remedies for their dissatisfaction;

- make every effort to ensure that the health and safety of our customers, as well as the quality of their environment, will be sustained or enhanced by our products and services; and

- assure respect for human dignity in products offered, marketing, and advertising; and respect the integrity of the culture of our customers.

Employees

We believe in the dignity of every employee and in taking employee interests seriously. We therefore have a responsibility to:

- provide jobs and compensation that improve workers' living conditions;

- provide working conditions that respect each employee's health and dignity;

- be honest in communications with employees and open in sharing information, limited only by legal and competitive constraints;

- listen to and, where possible, act on employee suggestions, ideas, requests and complaints;

- engage in good faith negotiations when conflict arises;

- avoid discriminatory practices and guarantee equal treatment and opportunity in areas such as gender, age, race, and religion;

- promote in the business itself the employment of differently abled people in places of work where they can be genuinely useful;

- protect employees from avoidable injury and illness in the workplace;

- encourage and assist employees in developing relevant and transferable skills and knowledge; and

- be sensitive to the serious unemployment problems frequently associated with business decisions, and work with governments, employee groups, other agencies and each other in addressing these dislocations.

Owners /Investors

We believe in honoring the trust our investors place in us. We therefore have a responsibility to:

- apply professional and diligent management in order to secure a fair and competitive return on our owners' investment;

- disclose relevant information to owners/investors subject to legal requirements and competitive constraints;

- conserve, protect, and increase the owners/investors' assets; and

- respect owners/investors' requests, suggestions, complaints, and formal resolutions.

Suppliers

Our relationship with suppliers and subcontractors must be based on mutual respect. We therefore have a responsibility to:

- seek fairness and truthfulness in all of our activities, including pricing, licensing, and rights to sell;

- ensure that our business activities are free from coercion and unnecessary litigation;

- foster long-term stability in the supplier relationship in return for value, quality, competitiveness and reliability;

- share information with suppliers and integrate them into our planning processes;

- pay suppliers on time and in accordance with agreed terms of trade; and

- seek, encourage and prefer suppliers and subcontractors whose employment practices respect human dignity.

Competitors

We believe that fair economic competition is one of the basic requirements for increasing the wealth of nations and ultimately for making possible the just distribution of goods and services. We therefore have a responsibility to:

- foster open markets for trade and investment;

- promote competitive behavior that is socially and environmentally beneficial and demonstrates mutual respect among competitors;

- refrain from either seeking or participating in questionable payments or favors to secure competitive advantages;

- respect both tangible and intellectual property rights; and

- refuse to acquire commercial information by dishonest or unethical means, such as industrial espionage.

Communities

We believe that as global corporate citizens we can contribute to such forces of reform and human rights as are at work in the communities in which we operate. We therefore have a responsibility in those communities to:

- respect human rights and democratic institutions, and promote them wherever practicable;

- recognize government's legitimate obligation to the society at large and support public policies and practices that promote human development through harmonious relations between business and other segments of society;

- collaborate with those forces in the community dedicated to raising standards of health, education, workplace safety and economic well-being;

- promote and stimulate sustainable development and play a leading role in preserving and enhancing the physical environment and conserving the earth's resources;

- support peace, security, diversity and social integration;

- respect the integrity of local cultures; and

- be a good corporate citizen through charitable donations, educational and cultural contributions, and employee participation in community and civic affairs.

Caux Round Table (CRT) Contact Information:

For copies of the *Principles for Business* or further information, please visit the Caux Round Table web site at www.cauxroundtable.org, or contact one of the following CRT Secretariats or the Minnesota Center for Corporate Responsibility at:

Europe:
Maarten de Pous
Secretariat

Japan:
Yasushi Suda
Secretariat

United States:
Stephen B. Young
Secretariat

Minnesota Center for Corporate Responsibility
*Now known as the Center for Ethical Business Cultures (CEBC).
Web: www.cebcglobal.org

Appendix 5

CRITICAL ROLE OF THE CORPORATION IN A GLOBAL SOCIETY
A POSITION PAPER OF THE CAUX ROUND TABLE (CRT)

Overview

The CRT was launched in 1986 by senior business leaders from Europe, Japan and North America to play an important role in improving economic and social conditions in the world. Initially concerned to promote solutions to the tensions arising from trade imbalances, the CRT has monitored the continuing changes in the economic and political landscape, and its influence has grown through the formulation and worldwide circulation of its *Principles for Business*.

From its inception the CRT has been a values-based organization. It exists to promote principled business leadership and responsible corporate practice on the basis of jointly held values reflected in those Principles. It is now expanding to become a worldwide organization.

Global business stands at the crossroads of the fundamental changes taking place in the world. The CRT believes that business has a crucial role in helping to identify and promote solutions to issues that impede the development of a society that is more prosperous, sustainable and equitable.

Globalization is moving forward relentlessly, with freer movement of people, capital, jobs, trade and information. Global businesses operate in essentially a borderless manner and have considerable power to effect change, while the direct role of nation states internationally is diminishing. This leads to the development of 'soft' laws, i.e. the effect of international conventions and bilateral treaties being used by NGO's as representing society's expectations of conduct, in advance of their adoption into the laws of individual nation states. As reluctant as some corporations have traditionally been to go beyond their operational objectives, the time has come for the roles of corporations, governments and other institutions to be significantly redefined - a time for new partnerships and greater cooperation on a global level.

Need for Dialogue on the Role of the Corporation

The CRT believes that there is an urgent need for a sustained dialogue, initially among senior business leaders from around the world, and then including leaders of governments and other institutions, to define the critical role of the corporation in a global society. The rules are changing. Whether in the physical, social or economic environment, business leaders can no longer rely solely on past traditions, established strategies or earlier expectations of society.

To enable such a dialogue to be fruitful, the CRT proposes the following framework and beliefs, based on its *Principles for Business:*

- Corporations must be increasingly responsive to issues affecting the physical, social and economic environments not only because of their impact on business performance but also out of a pro-active sense of responsibility to all constituencies served.

- Corporations need to consider the balance between the short-term interests of shareholders and the longer-term interests of the enterprise and all its stakeholders.

- The primary responsibility of the corporation is to conduct its operations proficiently, i.e., to be technologically innovative, competitive and financially sound.

- Meeting traditional objectives and performance criteria however is not sufficient. Voluntary standards which exceed the requirements of prevailing law and regulations are necessary to the development of sustainable practices. Society's "license or franchise to operate" has to be earned.

- Corporations should lead by example through business practices that are ethical and transparent, and that reflect a commitment to human dignity, political and economic freedoms, and preservation of the planet.

- Corporations cannot act alone but should seek to address key societal issues through cooperative efforts with governments, other institutions and local communities. In such a dialogue, the CRT believes that the following issues should be given precedence:

- Trust and Transparency

- Wider Environmental Issues

- Haves/Have Nots—and the Employment Dilemma

These issues need to be examined in the context of the fundamental social, economic, political and technological changes taking place throughout the world today.

Global Economic and Political Environment

Some commentators suggest that we are at a major turning point in history - a time that occurs only once every hundred years or so, when adequate vision is lacking, leadership is weak, new technology sweeps across nations, gaps widen between people, laws and institutions break down, values weaken, crime and corruption increase, and human relations falter. Such factors inherently threaten world peace, stability and prosperity, while business globalization is accelerating in both the historically major economies and the strong new economies.

The period since the CRT was founded has encompassed the completion of the GATT agreement, strongly endorsed by CRT participants, and the formation of the WTO. Other developments include the completion of the Single European Market, the formation of NAFTA and the ASEAN agreements.

The collapse of communism in Central and Eastern Europe has created both opportunities and challenges. The emergence of India and China as major economies, together with the explosive growth of the Tiger economies, has generated unprecedented prosperity and industrial muscle. The emergence of market economies challenges expanding global businesses to help to enable those markets to reach their potential and to enhance the prosperity of their populations.

Threats to a prosperous and sustainable society include the gulf between rich and poor both within nations and between the successfully industrialized nations and their less developed neighbors. Social unrest and discontent are increased by deprivation, inequalities, religious fanaticism and organized crime. Unlawful migration is a destabilizing influence as those without money, jobs, knowledge or opportunity are attracted to centers of prosperity. Rapid population increases in many regions outstrip available resources and the possibilities of industrial development.

Business leaders rightly see major opportunities for access to new markets, for the wider utilization of intellectual property and technology, and for new investment. But they are also faced with formidable challenges to reduce the attendant risks and to promote the conditions for progress in the least developed countries.

Public Awareness and Scrutiny

The same period has seen a revolution in communications, itself the source of huge new global business operations. With easier and more immediate access to information, and the stimulus of media analysis, public interest in the conduct of business has intensified. Sophisticated media presentation focuses particular issues and heightens concern, especially where perceptions develop that the public interest is threatened or power is being abused.

Demands increase for greater transparency and for effective public scrutiny. Society expects corporations to be accountable, not just in traditional areas of financial performance, but across all functions that impact on the physical, social and economic environments.

Society's confidence is undermined by ignorance and suspicion but reinforced by information and understanding. Without confidence and trust, society can be expected to review its "license" or "franchise" for business to operate. It exercises its sanction through legislation and regulations, the operation of choice in the market place, actions of pressure groups, and corrosive public criticism of targeted sectors, corporations or key position holders.

Recent campaigns on top executive compensation, environmental performance, employment conditions, sale of arms, and customer service standards provide evidence of the potentially harmful effects of public alienation. Conversely, companies that have addressed the challenges openly have been able to win public support even while undertaking major changes involving restructuring, adoption of new technologies sometimes seen as threatening, and in resolving highly controversial issues such as disposal of toxic waste.

Increasingly, competitive advantage and customer loyalty are achieved through providing access and dialogue and demonstrating genuine concern for the needs of communities and the public interest.

The Physical Environment

Business has increasingly faced these challenges in regard to its effects on the physical environment and its sustainability. It is in this arena that issues have become most globalized and that intergovernmental conventions and NGOs have had significant influence. This has reshaped national legislation around the world, led to the formation of new international institutions, and had a huge impact on the policies and practices of businesses and their representative organizations. There are few remaining international corporations that have not published statements of environmental policy (as well as safety and health policy) while significant sectors have adopted a coherent voluntary worldwide code of responsible practice. Considerable progress has been made in disclosure and in introducing reporting and verification procedures.

Although many aspects of environmental concern still await scientific verification, the concept of a voluntary precautionary approach has evolved, coupled with significant public commitments on performance goals. (However, this pro-active move has also led to public concerns about truthfulness and trustworthiness - for instance in regard to spurious claims of "environmental friendliness," misleading eco-labeling and other attempts to establish unsubstantiated competitive advantage or consumer preference.)

Science and new technology have enabled business to take many beneficial initiatives - not least in efficient agriculture, safe water and hygienic food processing. However, maturing public attitudes introduce new challenges in terms of what is acceptable in the public interest. The adoption of unfamiliar risks raises deep public concern.

Important examples include the application of bio-technology and pesticides in agriculture and of additives and radiation in food preservation. Business must make both practical and ethical decisions on the adoption of risk, its assessment and effective communication with its constituencies.

The Social Environment

Population growth, unemployment, extremes between rich and poor, public health, migration flows and social disorder interact to affect the conditions in which business develops. The prevailing political framework determines whether the responses are subject to command economy rule, to free market economies or to something in between.

Education and training are the precursor to economic development, and most political regimes give these high priority. However, the resources required to ensure efficient delivery may be inadequate, depending upon the general economic climate and social infrastructure.

A natural consequence of successful business activity is that employment opportunities and wealth are created together with an increasingly cohesive and supportive social fabric. Successful business however, depends upon its efficiency, competitiveness and its flexibility to adapt to changes in the marketplace. For survival in the global market even the most enduring businesses have to adapt, through measures affecting employment levels and disposition. Significant factors include changes in demand, new technology and the arrival of new competition.

The Key Global Issues for Business

All of these developments have far-reaching consequences. Some favor business and others threaten it, but none can be ignored. The CRT affirms that the primary purpose of the corporation is to manage its business effectively. In doing so, however, global business cannot assert that "the only business of business is business." It should seize the opportunity to be an active participant in contributing to greater stability, prosperity and sustainability.

Many business leaders have recognized the implications of globalization for their corporations and have given increasing attention to the concerns addressed in this paper. A broadening consensus has developed that business has a responsibility towards the communities it serves and depends upon, to contribute beyond the strict requirements of the law, and beyond the needs of self-protection. Participants in the CRT affirm this perspective, and seek to define the responsibility of global corporations in relation to the following key issues:

1. Trust and Transparency

Business has a duty to the rest of society to be trustworthy and transparent in its dealings. Public suspicion of business motives and behavior is a negative influence which can lead to restrictive legislation and can threaten job creation and other potential benefits to society. A loss of trust may result in a virtual revocation of business's "license" or "franchise" to operate in the public interest. Communications technology and the media intensify the call for information and explanation. To obtain trust, worldwide business practices must satisfy the perceptions of society as to what is ethical. Global businesses should not participate in or condone bribery, money laundering or other corrupt practices but should take the lead, in cooperation with others, to eliminate them. In general, to exhibit the transparency that renews trust, business needs to be more proactive in sharing its aims with the public and must be ready to be audited on its principles and policies.

Some of the key steps to be taken include the following:

- Removing obstacles to greater openness and transparency;

- Adopting more proactive measures to achieve public understanding of the standards of business and its performance; and

- Decisively eliminating bribery and corruption despite the diversity of cultures and practices.

2. Wider Environmental Issues

Despite current efforts to address issues of sustainability of the physical environment, a new urgency is needed to protect the resources of our planet for future generations.

The CRT believes that shorter-term performance criteria have to be balanced against longer-term considerations involving the effects of business on its environments and thus its sustainability. While laws and conventions focus particular provisions for the conduct of business, attitudes, standards and practices must exceed legal requirements. Business needs to monitor the impact of its products and services and to stand for values with which society will identify.

Serious attention must also be given to developing sustainable practices and values with respect to the social environment. Extending the practice of many corporations which already publish their general principles for the conduct of their business, and of a large number which publish their policies and performance in areas of safety, health, the physical environment and energy efficiency, business should define its role in areas such as:

- Resource Management

- Technology Transfer

- Illicit Substances and Their Abuse

- The Family

- Encouragement of Sound Values in Society

Business must proactively participate in determining the extent and scope of its responsibility in such sensitive areas and the right relationship with other institutions involved.

3. Haves/Have-Nots—and the Employment Dilemma

It is not acceptable for the benefits of technology and innovation to bypass large sections of humankind. By pursuing the necessary conditions for free trade and foreign investment, business will be able to create the economic activity that will result in growing employment, an absolute condition for a prosperous country. Free trade and foreign investment done responsibly can make poor countries richer, make rich countries more efficient, accelerate the creation of wealth, create jobs, and finally produce a higher and more equitable worldwide standard of living.

Global business leaders and their counterparts in government must draw from past successes to develop policies that promote job creation, review regulatory constraints that inhibit job creation, and consider new risk-sharing between business and government. Above all, business leaders need to identify the factors which promote creativity and innovation and inspire confidence in enterprise rather than protectionism.

The CRT has addressed the need for job creation regularly during the past three years. It involves a complex set of issues with far-reaching implications both in industrialized and developing nations.

Resolution of the global employment dilemma may be fundamental to reducing risks of social upheaval and to finding solutions to other key global issues. One of the greatest strengths of business has been and must continue to be job creation, even as restructuring of current activities continues. Country after country has decided that increased private sector employment is the lynchpin to sustainable economic growth. The CRT believes that business has a responsibility to provide working conditions that respect each employee's health and dignity, and to provide jobs and compensation that improve the living conditions of workers and their families. But crucial factors must be addressed:

- Business must clarify and define its role in promoting job creation;

- Business must promote flexibility and employability;

- Business must seek to change regulations which inhibit change in employment practices or impose administrative burdens that threaten competitive employment; and

- Business must help to develop plans to assist those without jobs

Within a wider social and economic context, business together with other social partners also needs to address:

- The gulf between rich and poor within nations and between successfully developed and less developed economies;

- The urgent need in developing nations for a rule of law that honors contracts, protects both tangible and intellectual property, preserves human and worker rights, and requires enterprise accountability. Business also needs to support the development of a necessary infrastructure, the nurturing of a new work ethic and other measures to assure sustainable development of these emerging market economies; and

- The impact of increased migration and freer trade agreements upon all sectors of societies within both developed and developing nations.

Commitment to Effective Partnerships

The CRT believes that solutions to these and other complex global issues require the sustained cooperative efforts of business, government, and other institutions. Working alone, these powerful players are likely to fail. Working together, they can apply local models to international situations and find multifaceted solutions to complex problems. The partnership developed in many cities where businesses collaborate with local authorities, central government, education, emergency services and special interest groups could be adapted to global initiatives. Although the difficulties in achieving effective, lasting collaboration are likely to be daunting, business needs to take the initiative and persevere in this process.

Business must:

- Develop a coherent strategy for addressing global problems;
- Establish a constructive business network embracing its principal world centers;
- Develop dialogue with relevant public institutions;
- Mount and fund agreed initiatives and action programs; and
- Monitor and review progress and outcomes.

The Role of the CRT

Building on past achievements, the CRT is committed to be an active catalyst for principled business leadership. In particular the CRT will:

- Continue to widen the circle of senior business leaders around the world who share its vision and convictions and are ready to devote time and resources to finding the necessary answers;

- Initiate and sustain dialogues with leaders of governments and other institutions to develop common goals and values; and

- Seek to better define the critical role of the corporation in a global society and the new type of cooperation needed among business, governments and other concerned parties that will result in a vastly improved quality of life for the great majority of people in the world.

As its dialogues with enlightened leaders from business and other sectors lead to greater consensus, the CRT intends to issue Commitment Papers on the issues discussed in the Position Paper.

For more information about the

Center for Ethical Business Cultures CEBC

Visit our web site:

www.cebcglobal.org

Wilfred (Bill) Bockelman has forged a lifetime career in theology and journalism. He received a Masters of Journalism from Columbia University's Graduate School of Journalism. In addition to several books and numerous magazine articles on religious subjects he has also developed an interest in business and ethics. He was the founder and for 14 years the editor of a newsletter, *The Eye of the Needle: The Responsible Use of Wealth, Power and Position.* He is currently working on a book that combines his interests, *On the 8th Day God Created Money.*

To order additional copies of this book,
please send full amount plus $4.00 for
postage and handling for the first book and
50¢ for each additional book.

Send orders to:

Galde Press, Inc.
PO Box 460
Lakeville, Minnesota 55044-0460

Credit card orders call 1–800–777–3454
Phone (952) 891–5991 • Fax (952) 891–6091
Visit our website at http://www.galdepress.com

Write for our free catalog.